I invite you to do some mirror
with a simple affirmation "I love you.'
anything else you want to say to yourself or new belief you want to
engrain. Now the trick is to look deep into your eyes as you say the
affirmation to yourself. At first it might feel strange or uncomfortable,
but just keep going.

7. <u>Service Is an Act of Self-Love</u>

Spirit is in service to us all. To be alive is a blessing. The greatest
gift we can give in this life is to be of service to others. To be able to be
of service, and to give, is to show that you have more than enough. That
you are abundant and prosperous. There is no other feeling like giving
from your heart—to help someone else in need, and to be able to uplift
someone's spirit.

When you think about being in service to others and think about
the time that someone has helped you, and how that made you feel, that's
the same feeling you're giving to someone else when you're in service to
others. It doesn't cost anything to be kind. Offering a helping hand goes
farther than you'll ever know. To love others is to love yourself. Because
we're all connected, an act of kindness to someone else is ultimately an
act of kindness towards yourself. Love is abundant and the most
powerful thing in the world. So, when you're being of service and giving
love, you're literally making the world a better place. And you get to live
in this better place.

Now there are caveats to this. Ones that I, again, had to learn the
hard way. Being a heart centered human being is a gift, a blessing, but can
also be a liability. I would never change the nature of my heart, for she is
pure and true. However, my heart's ever-loving nature and desire to help
others has also put me in positions that ended up with me compromising
myself. One of the greatest lessons I learned from my NXIVM
experience was "discernment." Living life from a selfless and caring lens
is beautiful and truly rare. This is the essence of the angelic realm. It is a
quality that sets people apart. It's easy to be selfish, self-motivated, self-
focused, but to sacrifice, to care for others, that's where the magic lives.

169

THE UNTOUCHABLE JESSICA JOAN

The Downfall of NXIVM

JESSICA JOAN

Copyright © 2023 Jessica Joan
All rights reserved.
ISBN:979-8-218-27504-4

DEDICATION

Grandma Pasing, My Ancestors, Mama Gaia and The Silent Children.

"Keith Raniere thought women were weak, but it was the inherent strength and sense of personal responsibility exhibited by the women like Jess who testified against him that ultimately brought him to justice. Jess's testimony reflected her tremendous bravery and resilience. She recognized the signs of exploitation in a way few could and managed to escape before being assaulted and to protect others as well."

- **Moira Penza**
(Assistant US Attorney of the Eastern District of New York for the NXIVM trial)

Table of Contents

About the Author

Jessica Joan is an evolutionary storyteller from Southern California. She identifies as a Pacific Islander with her lineage spanning from Filipino, Spanish, Chinese, and much more. Jessica is an artist dedicated to using her life experience and talents to help heal the collective consciousness and to move it forward.

Growing up in an unconventional and chaotic environment, Jessica experienced severe trauma, which afforded her the gift to deeply empathize with humanity, as well as provided her with the burning desire to help others heal. Jessica started this journey at the age of 5 after her mother abandoned the family. The gravity of Jessica's emotional pain opened her up in a way that led her down many roads searching to fill that void. Through her many trials and tribulations, she has learned to become masterful at alchemizing her trauma into unconditional love.

Nowadays, Jessica lives life fully by allowing her Higher Self and gut intuition to lead her on her journey. In part, Jessica is able to enhance her life through exploring her first artistic love of poetry, which she began writing as a child as a means to express her profound pain and emotion. Jessica's captivating smile and presence landed her modeling jobs alongside some of the biggest lifestyle brands. At the same time, Jessica gravitated to the craft of acting. In addition to acting, Jessica added "Executive Producer" to her resume for her role in her first project "gLOVEs" which she also starred in—a short film based off her original poem and filmed in France with Director Hugo Valentine.

"Evolutionary Storyteller" is a term coined by Jessica, which is defined by the intention to use her art and share her life experiences to help people evolve. Intention is at the forefront of everything Jessica does, from her activism and desire to fight for what's right to gazing back into her heritage, as a descendent of warriors. Jessica's plans are centered on speaking truth to the uncomfortable subjects, especially those society avoids, as well as speaking for those who do not have a voice.

Jessica is a survivor, a warrior and a bridge who is here to show others they can overcome even the most devastating experiences and return back to love.

Foreword

My name is Jessica Joan, and this is my story of transformation, which led me to becoming the linchpin that took down Keith Raniere and the NXIVM cult. You may have seen the headlines, read the stories or even watched a few documentaries, but this is unlike any story you've ever heard before.

I'm a firm believer that everything happens for a reason. I'm not a victim. I'm a survivor, a warrior, and to be frank, this experience was no accident. In my mind, coincidences only happen if you aren't aware enough to see the lesson and the bigger picture. This requires guidance and intention to recognize. Ultimately, we are creations of a supremely intelligent and unconditionally loving Universe, but this Universe is also quite ironic and has a brilliant sense of humor. Sometimes the Universe may lead us towards pain, but ultimately it is our choice to become resilient.

After all, what is life without some tears and earth-shattering heartbreaks? Or, for that matter, pee-in-your-pants laughter and a reassuring kiss on the forehead? This is how Spirit works. My childhood was filled with a whole spectrum of severe traumas, from parents struggling with substance abuse, abandonment, to sexual abuse. I'm baring my soul and putting it all on the table because ever since I was a little girl, I knew that my story was meant to be shared.

Deep down inside, I knew that my soul chose this experience, and that I had the will to do it. It has been an overwhelming and daunting feeling of responsibility to carry. Of course, I struggled with this responsibility and what felt like a burden for most of my life. I wasn't ready to answer the call until I started to heal my deepest trauma and come out of the other end ready to fight.

I am deeply human but have always been guided by the Divine. When you are a child and experience the deepest pain imaginable, it makes it hard to smile. Despite the torment I experienced, I have always kept my love intact. My heart has been through the wringer more times than I can count, but I have always trusted in my intuition. It always told me to fight, to keep going, and to believe that things would get better.

This is what my story is about: perseverance, courage, vulnerability and remembering your true, divine nature. I want to be clear that my pain does not make me special or unique, but my ability to "transmute" pain does. I know I'm not alone in feeling such devastating heartbreak, which is why I hope sharing my story helps even just one person find their way back to their truth.

The ultimate irony is that what I've been through is what led me to be someone who ended up enrolling in NXIVM's courses, and in the same breath, it led me to be the person who didn't let them harm me; ultimately, I became the person who took them down. But before I take you on this journey, here are some of the facts:
I was the first woman to leave "The Vow" (aka DOS), the woman's only secret society. Secondly, I was not branded, nor did I engage in any sexual activity with Keith Raniere. And lastly, I am 1 of 2 "Jane Does" behind Keith Raniere's indictment, which led to his arrest in Mexico (I'm "Jane Doe 2," in case you're curious).

Preface

The sum of my experience in NXIVM was like waking up in a nightmare where you are the main character of a suspense thriller movie only to realize it wasn't a movie—it was your real life. It was my worst nightmare come to life, where my LA, ego-persona had accidentally fallen into a cult where the leader wanted to have sex with me. How fucking cliché. The beginning of my journey with NXIVM was like pressing down on the gas and going 100 mph the whole time, without ever taking my foot off the pedal. To call it an "experience" is a huge understatement. It has been a whole spiritual undertaking that included my call and initiation into *The Hero's Journey* a la Joseph Campbell.

Through NXIVM, I got what I was seeking: elevation and enlightenment. Those lessons, however, were not delivered through the courses or the promises of ESP, which their convincing presentations led me to believe was possible only through entering their organization. Rather, it was actually breaking out of NXIVM, and their control, and not allowing my Spirit to be manipulated that led me to the enlightenment that I was seeking. Through fighting for my freedom, I actually got what I was looking for.

Somewhere along my journey, I descended into a space where an ego death was necessary. It left me with nothing but my truth. My truth was that everything I needed was already inside me: my courage, my will, and my bravery, and they were all tested. This activated my true care for human fragility while also exposing mine in a profound way. There was no turning back. It feels like my whole life prepared me for that moment and was divinely guided every step of the way. It wasn't just "Jessica"; it was a Higher Power showing me the way in and the way out. It was a job I know I was destined to do, and I'm so honored and grateful to have been able to do what I did. Without a doubt, it showed me who I really am.

When everything fell apart, it seemed as though my plans had been derailed. The irony is my experience in NXIVM allowed me to be the master of my own destiny by remembering to trust myself. What my journey and experience taught me is that all the answers exist within me. It is my job to quiet the noise and listen to what my gut is telling me. Through this experience, I learned to trust my intuition, follow my heart and allow my instincts to guide me.

An important awareness, especially for big, openhearted, giving people, is to understand that, just because you think, feel, and behave in a certain way, doesn't mean someone else does.

Discernment (*noun*)- "the ability to judge well."

Before I learned discernment, I was constantly operating from a place of thinking that people had the same level of care and depth for me as I did for them. But I was wrong. This left me feeling sad, abandoned, taken for granted and a whole plethora of other things that didn't align with me. I just didn't understand. I would repeat this cycle many times, over and over again, and I kept attracting the same kinds of people and similar situations. This also stemmed from my lack of self-love and self-respect, which I didn't learn until much later in life.

Due to my chaotic and dysfunctional upbringing, I didn't have the tools or role models to show me the love I deserved, so I ended up having a high tolerance for abuse and mistreatment. In fact, I was abused. Although tragic, these painful lessons early on helped serve me in handling the NXIVM situation. My open heart, innocence and belief in goodness attracted me to the organization. This, on top of my deep wounds and wanting to belong and to have deep emotional connections with people were the keys to opening the door.

Here are some things I live by:

"Whatever you can confront, you can overcome."

"Every moment is a chance for anything to happen."

"Sometimes you have to let good things go, so great things can happen."

"Serenity in aloneness is among the greatest powers you can attain."

"It is what it is."

"If you're not growing, you're dying."

"It's not enough to be alive if you're not actually living."

My Ordinary World

My childhood was not a Cinderella story. It was, in fact, the opposite: a reverse Cinderella story, if you will. Growing up, my parents were together and, on the outside, I had what would seem to be a beautiful, secure and privileged upbringing. The floors were covered in marble with a chandelier floating above the doorway. Baby bottles were filled with precious Evian water. My parents celebrated my birth with a steak and lobster dinner in the hospital, and I was brought home from the hospital in a limo. That's how I was ushered into the world. Above all, I was born well-loved, adored and cared for. This charmed life was sadly short-lived, and any dream for a normal childhood would be just that: a dream.

Sometimes dreams can turn into nightmares.

CUT TO: EXT. SUSPECT'S HOUSE

The SWAT team, on the front steps, prepares to blow the front door off of its hinges. We hear a roaring BOOM as the door goes flying into the living room.

SWAT

Everybody on the ground!!!

And there I was, a little girl wrapped in a towel, with my wet hair dripping warm water down my shoulders—only to be frozen in fear. My cousin, with a microphone in hand, had been belting out "Lucky" by Britney Spears on our family cd player. She was cut short by yells from the SWAT team. In that one moment, my life suddenly changed, and I was no longer dreaming. I began a life that only seemed to exist in movies.

*

Ever since I was a little girl, I've been adventurous and fearless. When my parents were still together—during the "good part" of my childhood—I lived in a neighborhood filled with friends and had a lot of freedom to ride my Barbie bike around. When the sun was out, it was warm, but not blazing hot. I wore hard, rubber bottom-soled, Velcro chunky sandals. One day, my neighborhood best friend Gabby came over to tell me something about abandoned bunnies. This was told to me in a shy, almost half-anxious way. There was an urgency written on her face. "The bunnies are out there," she said.

Corona Ranch is the nicer part of the Inland Empire, a non-descript suburban town in California. It's dry and desolate with some strip malls. It's a city lined with newly built track homes. On the road towards the end of my cul-de-sac, there was a low-walled desert alley with a makeshift entrance barrier made of sandbags. It wasn't much to look at, except for some weeds, dried desert plants and sand embankments.

Pedaling hard, I ditched my bike at the entryway, which formed a dirt path. We traversed a little rocky plain that led us to a hole where the abandoned baby bunnies were huddled together, neatly arranged and waiting for their mother who was never to return. We made the decision to bring them home. Biking back to my house, I was confronted by my frantic and frightened parents. They were worried sick about me when I had not come back. In my mind, I wasn't concerned or worried at all, knowing I had done a noble thing. My parents did not share that sentiment, but they were relieved that I was home. Nothing mattered—I just knew we needed to save the baby bunnies.

*

This call to adventure and desire to protect others became a reoccurring theme in my life, one that eventually took me to Albany and NXIVM.

But before we go down that rabbit hole. . .

Little Jess had many more adventures and roadblocks to overcome throughout her childhood. My mother was a nurse, and she specifically treated children with ailments and babies born prematurely. She was beautiful, charismatic, and always made people feel like they were the most special person in the world. My mom had a privileged upbringing; her father was financially well-off and would have provided her anything she wanted, but she was a rebel by nature and wanted to do everything her way, on her terms. She even got married to my dad in secret. She went to nursing school and graduated at the top of her class. She was also a natural born hustler. She worked her graveyard nursing shifts until the eighth month of her pregnancy with me, when she was forced to take maternity leave as per her boss's orders. My mom was 22 and my dad was 21 when I was born. They were effectively children raising children.

She was always on her feet, a quality she passed down to me. In fact, it was so chaotic, I ended up getting toxemia while I was still in the womb. Even before I was born, there was never any peace. I honestly attribute a lot of this to my inherent state of restlessness, which is why my inner peace is of the utmost importance. I would often visit my mom at work as a little girl. My favorite thing to do was to get into the crib with the children there; there was one girl in particular, around my age who had cancer. She told me I was her best friend. I brought her toys, and read her stories.

Although I spent a lot of time with my mom, I was definitely a daddy's girl. That could be due to the fact that he took me to Toys R' Us every day and seldom told me "no." I was his first born and he loved nothing more than to take care of me. He was an entrepreneur with his own landscaping business. My mom used to tell me, "Your dad is very smart and could do just about anything he put his mind to." They were both very protective of me, so they didn't trust anyone to watch me. Therefore, my dad ran his landscaping business so he could take care of me from home. This version of my parents went on for a few years.

My mom had her own demons even though she was outwardly a sweet person. For as much virtue as she had, internally she was corrupted, narcissistic, and generally did whatever she wanted no matter what bodies she left behind. From moment to moment, she could go from "Mom of the Year" to solely fulfilling her own need for chaos and self-medication. The consequences of my mom being this way left Little Jess alone, heartbroken, confused and left to fend for herself.

Fortunately, I was not totally left on my own; I had my dad, but he had demons, too. One demon that they shared was the "Meth Monster," AKA "crystal," "crank," "ice"—it goes by many names and can show up in many forms, in many places, like the Devil who doesn't discriminate in seducing his victims. This monster fills people with euphoria, makes them feel invincible, and momentarily melts away the pain. What they don't realize is that they're selling their soul. Meth demands more and more—it's never satiated—until it has taken all a person loves, and anything left of them is soul-less.

While my parents were on drugs, they began to spiral. Their spiral took away my first childhood dream to become a model. Eventually, because the drugs got the best of them, my dream, and the life that they had built, started to crumble. My parents were putting me in competitive modeling castings, and I was offered to sign with a huge agency as a child. The agents told my mother, "If you focus on your daughter, you won't need to work another day in your life." Unfortunately, we started to miss meetings and castings, and soon this opportunity disappeared and faded, as my parents dove deeper into their addiction.

*

Amidst the chaos, my parents still managed to become parents to two new children, my sister and my brother. I was so excited to be a big sister. They were so small, but my parents were more present with their drug abuse than they were with us, so my siblings weren't able to get the attention they needed from our parents. Because I was older, I experienced our mom actually being a mom, whereas to my siblings, my mother would become a face that would soon become a stranger. My little brother once asked my sister if she had a picture of our mom because he had forgotten what she looked like.

My brother wasn't even out of diapers before my mom left us, choosing drugs over her family. Abandoned. But even before then, my mom was already neglectful, leaving us kids to our own devices. Soon, the house became chaotic as my parents were always fighting. Fighting was the new norm, the new language, the new reality. Their fighting left us invisible. Our cries for attention went unnoticed as our walls were scribbled with crayon markings—seeking their attention, but not receiving any—even amidst a symphony of our cries, which filled the halls, to no avail. With no parents around to care for my siblings, I was no longer a child, but forced to take on the role of a caretaker.

Eventually, the fighting led to my parents' separation. My dad was in and out, and if it wasn't for the love of my grandparents, this story would have taken an even darker turn. After my mom left, my dad came back to the rescue and raised his three children on his own. We ended up moving in with my aunt, my dad's sister, and her three children. There were six children now. Like Cinderella, this was the part of the story where I became a pumpkin at midnight.

My mom leaving shattered my heart into a million pieces. No longer happy-go-lucky, I was confronted by the feeling of not being loved. This broke me and eventually hardened me to the outside world. Whereas most children my age had the privilege of being care-free, supported, and nurtured to grow, I was changing my little brother's diapers, possessed by PTSD of abandonment, and would relentlessly page "911" on my mom's pager, begging her to come home and hoping this nightmare would come to an end.

I was afraid that my father would eventually leave us, too. Often times, I decided to take mustard and vinegar from the refrigerator and pour them into my dad's slippers so that he wouldn't leave the house. So many slippers were ruined. My thought process was that it would be impossible for him to take a step further—even stopping him from taking the garbage out into the driveway. He managed to complete his task by wearing my aunt's fuzzy slippers.

My experience growing up conditioned me to have a high pain threshold for trauma and abuse, particularly abandonment by my mother. My mom would leave—and come back—then leave—and come back again, although her absence was the reality. The experience of being abandoned was so normal for me that allowing myself to be manipulated and abused bled into every aspect of my life. This wasn't me being naïve; I was simply innocent. In my heart, I held a sincere belief and hope that my mom would come back, but she continued to break my heart into a million pieces over and over again.

After my mom left, my birthday became a sore subject for me. A time that was once joyous, happy and free had turned into one of the saddest days of the year. I would sleep away most of my birthday—no cake, no friends, no nothing. I would sleep until it was no longer my birthday. It never felt like my birthday was something to celebrate because my life was fractured, and even though I had the strength and will to continue on and move forward, my life just didn't feel like something to celebrate, especially because my mom would always promise to be there, but she never kept her word.

The first time my mother missed my birthday, she gave me a card later on to apologize. On the cover of the card was a cartoon dog writing on a chalkboard, like he was in detention, writing over and over, "I promise to never miss your birthday ever again." I took the card at face value, but sadly, she missed my birthday every year after that.

The heart is all-knowing and guides the way, regardless if we listen to it or not. There's a reason why people say, "The heart wants what the heart wants." Ultimately, the heart wants to love and be loved. Pain is also part of the natural experience of the heart, and it is also an important indicator that we often times overlook. Pain is the heart's signal, letting you know that something is awry and hurting you. This is where self-love comes into play. Most people don't realize that they really are not loving themselves. I was one of those people.

Loving yourself has become a cliché, but it is a cliché for a reason. "You can't love someone until you love yourself," or, "How you love yourself is how you teach others to love you." People associate this idea of love with romantic love, but it applies to everything—family, friendships, community, and yes, romance, too (but not exclusively). Most people want to receive all the fruits of what self-love, and what love in general, brings. What they don't realize is that it's a lot of hard fucking work. In the grand scheme of things, it really shouldn't be. But because we've grown up in a world and a society that has taught us the opposite of love, we've been conditioned in ways that we don't even realize.

Growing up, we think of our parents as superheroes. They are ideally who we look to on how to be, but also, they are our first pillar in understanding what love is. It's primal, it's natural and it's intuitive to hold this belief in our parents. If you're one of the lucky few who grew up with two loving parents, and were supported and felt safe, then you're blessed beyond measure. Now, for the rest of us, we have learned that our parents are not our superheroes, and for some of us, they may even be villains in our story. But the reality is that our parents are not superheroes, even if they seem perfect. They are simply people trying to figure out themselves in a world that doesn't teach you how to love yourself. This world is the opposite, in fact.

Being Filipino and growing up in that culture, family connection is of the utmost importance. We're told to respect our elders at all times, no matter what, even in light of their lack of deserving respect. Having respect for our elders and treating them with care is a good thing because our elders have wisdom. However, this rule is very destructive when the principle of respect overrules one's need for expression of one's truth. We repress our truth and feelings in order to uphold the family, and the principles, to our own demise. This is not self-love.

When my mom would leave, my heart would signal deep pain and longing for her, but also disappointment. Then, she would reappear and walk through the front door on her own accord, and my heart signaled a warning. I was weary of her, and I did not feel safe to love her, so I distanced myself, often refusing to talk to her. When I would express my feelings about my mom to my father, he would say, "Well, she's still your mom, so you need to respect her." This was the culture telling me what I needed to feel, how I needed to act, and how I needed to be. The truth is my heart was trying to protect me, and it knew what was right all along. Listening to my heart and my needs is the definition of self-love.

All I heard constantly were excuses and justifications. I was told that since she was my mom, I needed to respect her, no matter how much pain she caused me. I stopped listening to my heart because I listened to my dad, who I thought knew best for me. So many people do what their parents say, regardless of what they want or what they believe.

I put the walls of my heart down, and I let my mother back in. This toxic cycle and pattern of abuse continued many times over.

Ultimately, this cycle put my heart in peril, left on the side of the road for dead. My heart was silenced and neglected. Even at its lowest ebb, however, the heart still fights for you, and it always will. In ignoring my own heart, I did what I thought was necessary; I kept forgiving and allowing this emotional abuse, without protecting my heart and ultimately without protecting myself. Of course, forgiveness is important to healing and getting to the other side. However, forgiveness that goes against what's best for us—just for the sake of moving forward—is not self-love or kindness. It's not forgiveness when we say "I forgive you" and you're holding stuff inside, without processing the pain and getting to a place of letting go and surrender. Reclaiming one's power and not letting something outside of ourselves hurt us is forgiveness. Holding onto the thought and the feelings causes resentment and is a detriment towards us.

Similar to a Buddhist adage, we burn ourselves when we hold onto anger, like a hot stone in the palm of our hand; we have the intention of throwing it, but the pain sears the hand as you hold onto it. The pain can be put down, like placing a hot stone into the soothing, cooling, and calm stream of self-love. However, when you do not forgive, you're only burning yourself. The caveat to this is that you must truly be ready to let go and forgive, and to do the work necessary to put the stone down. Only then will forgiveness truly grant you freedom.

Forgiveness for forgiveness's sake is spiritual bypassing.

Spiritual bypassing (*noun*): "The tendency to use spiritual ideas and practices to side-step facing unresolved emotional issues, psychological wounds or unfinished developmental tasks."

In other words, thinking you're doing the work, without actually doing it. The result of spiritual bypassing, in terms of forgiveness, is abuse to oneself that enables abusers to continue to hurt you. You're moving forward without truly addressing the underlying issue, which is fundamentally unfair to yourself. You're repressing your true feelings, which can lead to resentment, anger, depression, and so much more.

Genuine forgiveness and openness is what allowed me to become as strong and resilient as I am today. In contrast, the forgiveness towards my mother as a child was not genuine or truthful—unknowingly, I was spiritual bypassing because my dad forced the idea of forgiving her upon me and, secondly, because deep inside, I really wanted to believe her.

This was not real forgiveness, because true forgiveness comes with changed behavior, boundaries, honesty, and clear communication; otherwise, it just perpetuates unhealthy and toxic behaviors.

At that point in time, my mother was not deserving of my forgiveness because she had no accountability, did not accept personal responsibility, and most importantly, did not change her behavior. When you forgive someone with the intention of allowing them back into your life, you're trusting that they will be better. You lay down boundaries with your understanding of self-love and express what you need to keep that self-love intact. Ultimately, the person you're letting back in has a responsibility to uphold if you're allowing them back into your life.

There's another version of forgiveness where the person you're forgiving lacks accountability, does not change their behavior, and does not take personal responsibility for their actions. When you practice this type of forgiveness, it is truly for your own well-being without harboring any negative feelings towards someone, but you're not going to allow them back in your life. This is where you simply forgive them for their actions, understanding that they are human, but with your wisdom of knowing who you are and that they are not going to add to your happiness, you lovingly let them go.

The greatest act of forgiveness is for oneself. Our innocence and our desire to love and be loved can put us in situations that lead us into harm's way. My belief is that all the pain and trauma that come along our path are no accident, but they were necessary lessons to return us to a deeper sense of self-love. Yet, there is still a fracture that occurs within oneself when we endure the pain of hard lessons.

We often blame others, but the real truth is that there's some blame and personal responsibility that we need to have for ourselves. If we knew better, we would have done better. We can't live in shame. We embrace these lessons as part of our growth in becoming the greatest version of ourselves. To claim personal responsibility is to claim our power, and in embracing all that has happened to us, we become free of it all.

Learning hard lessons is part of growth and understanding, but at the same time, with our new understanding, we gain a higher sense of self-awareness and learn to practice self-care, which is the whole point of these lessons. Hopefully these lessons prevent us from being further abused. However, there are specific situations that are purely evil, predatory and practically inescapable. Even gaining self-awareness and practicing self-care alone cannot stop situations that you truly do not have control over. Survivors of extreme domestic abuse, human trafficking, and child victims of sexual abuse, for example, do not choose to be victimized.

Survivors of extreme domestic abuse can be lured into a relationship under false pretenses (e.g., by narcissists) and, upon realizing the toxic nature of the relationship, they leave it, only to have the abuser harass and stalk them. A relentless abuser can take such extreme measures so that mere self-awareness on the part of the survivor is not the answer. Survivors who have escaped human trafficking can have a similar experience, where their trafficker will hunt them down, no matter where they run. In those situations, it's important for the survivor to have help and support, to truly break free of these situations. Just like a child is purely innocent and only knows love, predators' prey on their innocence and trust. Children are not expected to be aware, and it is the job of the parents and the community at large to protect the most vulnerable beings, which are children. As a collective, the community must come together to support survivors in need of healing.

When we're children, we do not have self-awareness instilled into us because we're still learning about who we are. We're influenced by the world and our experiences, as well as the people around us. Over time, the patterns we find ourselves in, such as the choices and decisions we make, are part of a system of neural pathways in our brain, which we are building constantly, like laying down railroad tracks. For example, we may be told something is "wrong," or we may feel angry because we did not receive support from our parents, or we have a moment of trauma that fractures our experience. As a result, we may behave in response by overcompensating, or by self-soothing in ways that are disruptive and negative in order to survive and attempt to fill a void inside. Overindulgence, overspending, anger, poor communication, staying in toxic relationships, self-harm, addiction, self-sabotage, people pleasing, manipulating others, etc. are all examples of ways we self-soothe and compensate for not feeling whole.

As we accrue experiences and become familiar riding these tracks, the route becomes more and more defined. We become so familiar with these routes that we hop on the train unconsciously and continue business as usual, which is expressed through our unconscious behavior. Some of these tracks lead us towards self-actualizing desired destinations, while other tracks lead us astray and can be destructive toward our well-being (and the well-being of others). An example of a healthy, supportive track is one that is built by parents who love unconditionally, meaning that as we grow up, we feel self-confident and capable out in the real world as we are reassured of our self-worth. Perhaps you had a teacher in elementary school who recognized a special quality in you and pushed you to strive for more, to reach your higher potential by encouraging you; this can also lead a person towards a positive future where they can accomplish great things.

In contrast, a negative track is built out of fear, a feeling of lack, or a version of love that is abusive, but it feels like love because it's all we've ever known and it's what we understand love to be. One can become addicted to feeling pain, drama and chaos. Unknowingly, we actually seek out relationships and situations that mimic patterns of past abuse, mistaking it for love because we've never known what real love looks and feels like. We fall into the trap of victimhood because we are caught up in the experience of life, unconsciously riding that train. We relive these pains because it is part of a pattern that we built while forming the railroad tracks. On this ride, the route feels familiar to us, but it does not serve us and can ultimately put us in peril.

As adults, we are responsible for our choices to protect ourselves and be aware. When we find ourselves on a dangerous ride, we need to make a new track. The former railway that does not serve us fades into the background and is no longer used, while the new railway that does serve us becomes more and more defined. This is how we re-pattern old destructive behavior into new patterns with self-awareness, leading us to a desired destination: self-love, self-worth, and self-actualization.

Childhood trauma can also be used against you to prevent you from becoming who you really are. Lacking self-awareness, we risk staying in toxic cycles and abusive relationships, which we don't deserve. The Little Jess inside of me deserved so much better. My biggest pitfalls stemmed from my feelings of abandonment, in which I desperately sought out romantic relationships to fill that void, unable to see that these relationships were not truly serving me and were perpetuating more of the abandonment harm in the form of anxiety and avoidance. I was repressing my emotions and pain, while living a self-indulgent lifestyle to cope with the underlying issues. Growing up with a narcissistic mother who abandoned and neglected me, and who constantly offered promises she never delivered, deeply impacted my self-worth and created insecurities of not feeling like I was enough.

The NXIVM organization was able to use all the above to create a perfect storm that I almost drowned in. They were adept at preying on fears and past trauma, which became currency for the organization. They preyed on my light and goodness, as a means to lure me in, by disguising their evil intentions as a humanitarian personal development program. NXIVM was the umbrella name for an organization that was founded on a series of "educational" courses and curriculum, marketed to help like-minded individuals who desired to reach their highest human potential. It was an organization that attracted good people who had gone through difficult and challenging experiences in life, who wanted to heal that part of themselves to then help others heal their trauma, in order to change the world for the better.

The Runaway

The reverse Cinderella story had now become a dominant theme in my life. My mother battled with her drug addiction, but the Meth Monster won, and she slowly faded away from our lives, becoming a runaway to a different reality. My dad, on the other hand, rose to the occasion in her absence and did what he could to survive and to take care of his family. He joined forces with his younger sister because she was also a single parent, raising three children on her own. My aunt worked as an administrator in a hospital, while my dad needed to find a job that let him stay at home with the six children. We didn't have the financial resources to live comfortably on my aunt's salary, so eventually, my dad turned his own demons and addiction into becoming an entrepreneur in the narcotics industry. He was taking care of us, while simultaneously running his ever-growing drug enterprise with a fully-functioning meth lab in the back house.

All this sounds crazy to someone from the outside looking in, but this is what my life came to be. At some point, I learned to cope with the absence of my mother; it was a deep wound that was still bleeding and throbbing, but I managed to keep moving on while the infection persisted. Luckily, during this time, I was not alone, not just because of my siblings, but because of my three cousins. They sometimes say that people with nothing are the happiest, and with that, is the innocence and purity of when you have love and share commonality with a little community. That community was my family and the bonds between my siblings and I, as well as my cousins.

I regained a small part of my childhood while growing up alongside my cousins. We rode bikes and played freeze tag with the neighborhood children in our apartment complex. Despite all the chaos and unresolved trauma that would ensue, I was able to be distracted by the wholesome experiences of going outside and playing. My great-grandmother, "Grandma Pasing," and I were very close and connected to each other. She was the first person I ever truly, deeply loved. She was always by my side as a baby and, as I was experiencing a lot of abandonment, she was the rock and pillar that kept me going. She had nine children, smoked black cigarillos (backwards, ironically) and was a master at playing cards. She was an incredible woman and matriarch. We watched wrestling together. Her favorite was Shawn Michaels, "The Heartbreak Kid." She had a little crush on him. I spent my fifth-grade summer taking care of her, brushing her dentures and changing her commode. Sadly, she passed away when I was visiting my cousins in San Francisco. This was another huge fracture, deepening my feelings of abandonment.

In addition to the dozens of people in my life, I had numerous pets growing up. My father was very unattached to our pets; although he loved and cared for them, he did what had to be done. When we had to move, my dad didn't give me any notice. There was no real goodbye as he would send my pets to a loving home that could properly care for them, but being a small child, I couldn't understand that. I just felt my small furry friends were being taken away from me. I ended up with two Dalmatians at different times growing up: Jasmine and Jasmine #1. With moving, our dogs didn't come with us. Things that were close to me were always going away. This deeper instilled my belief that things I loved would eventually leave me.

When my mom ran away to her new life, feeding her demons, she also (coincidentally) became a drug "entrepreneur." Only my mom's enterprise was based in LA, and it became larger than my dad's business. She went into business with her new lover, a notorious kingpin in LA. Their operation ran across the country, from New York and New Jersey, where shipments of drugs were sent out and cash flowed back. A hustler by nature, she switched from nursing to drug dealing and applied the same work ethic from her previous job to her new one. Her story was very unorthodox—when you think about drug dealers, you think about people who come from a broken home, but she was a beautiful young woman with a nursing degree. She could have chosen any path; she definitely wasn't the typical drug dealer. Though my mother, on the outside, looked like her life was put together, in reality, her unresolved trauma led her on a path to ultimate destruction.

Growing up, each of my siblings had a "best friend" cousin—our partners in crime—who were each close in age. This time of my life was light in an otherwise very dark and depressing period. While my dad and aunt were preoccupied with work, we were left to our own devices, which basically consisted of adventures and managing to stay out of trouble. From playing Pokémon cards and having mud fights, to locking the youngest siblings in the closet for misbehaving, we were just children having some wholesome fun. The internet was just emerging, as AOL came onto the scene and the sound of dial-up connection meant access to a new world: the "World Wide Web." I may be aging myself right now, but this is just to tell you that I am part of the elder Millennial generation, the one who experienced the world pre-internet *and* post-internet. This was a time before Google, when we were more reliant on our own imaginations, had more meaningful in-person connections (without distraction from social media) and followed directions literally printed out from MapQuest.

For a few years, I grew up with my cousins under the same roof, until that fateful day when the SWAT team stormed our house and the peak of my childhood ended, coming to a crashing halt. Child Protective Services took us to Orangewood, which was a facility for children in need of foster care that offered programs to help young adults eventually become independent. There are so many horror stories about the foster care system, which often leaves children even more traumatized with negative experiences that set them up for an even harder life. That could have easily been my path had I not been blessed to end up at Orangewood, which was a beautiful and loving experience for me. It felt like summer camp; the people in charge of Orangewood were empathetic, caring, and helpful during this challenging transition in my life, having been taken away from my dad. I stayed at Orangewood for several months before my grandparents eventually adopted my siblings and me.

My grandmother, "Mama Pie," on my maternal side was generous and loving. She would help anyone in need and showed her love by feeding people she cared about, especially with delicious Filipino food. Everyone wanted to come over to her house just to taste her food, always cooked with love. "How are your parents? Are you hungry? Eat now! Eat now! More rice. You're too skinny."

My grandparents were Catholic, old-fashioned, led a conservative lifestyle, and were very concerned with what other people thought, so much so that they repressed the truth to avoid confronting challenging issues similarly to a lot of Asian cultures. When it came to my mom's drug abuse, my grandparents acted as if nothing was wrong. We never talked about her or how it affected us. By ignoring the issue entirely, they enabled my mother. Instead of holding her responsible or pushing her to be a better mother, my grandparents picked up the slack for her and raised us without my mother receiving any consequences or being expected to be accountable for anything. My grandmother simply loved my mother to a fault—there was no question about it.

My mom's stepdad, "Papa Frank," was Creole, grew up on the East Coast, was an ex-Navy officer and was a strong disciplinarian. He was so strict. He called the bathroom the "lavatory." He wouldn't let us put food in the garbage without putting it in a bag first to prepare the trash to be disposed of, which felt overly-regimented, but I later learned to appreciate his smart and efficient ways. When I was in fifth grade, I recall Papa Frank would make me take a nap every day at two o'clock (on the dot). In some ways, I felt like he ran the household like a ship deck. He even had old tattoos from his Navy days. Whenever he picked us up from elementary school in the minivan, and I had friends that needed a ride, he would intimidate people, such as by telling them to take off their hats as a sign of respect before they got in the car: "Were you raised in a barn?" he asked.

My grandparents were full of love. Though they were older, they embraced the responsibility of taking care of us children. I tried to make it as easy for them as I possibly could, which is when my natural leadership qualities began to form.

The registration for our elementary school contained enrollment papers in a large manila envelope that needed to be filled out for myself and my siblings. On my own initiative, I put together our forms, filled each of them out, and brought them gingerly to my grandparents to sign. By high school, however, I no longer even bothered getting their signature, which meant that all my "excused absence" notes were both written and signed by me consistently, so that I could skip the last hour of classes. School interfered with watching my favorite soap opera, "Passions," which went on at two o'clock, an hour before school ended.

When my grandparents first gained custody of us, they lived in the City of Orange, within Orange County. However, the schools that we attended required us to follow a dress code—to guard against students wearing gang-affiliated colors—not to be confused with the prep school uniforms depicted in *The O.C.* The reality is there's more to Orange County than just a beach town, trust fund kids, and Disneyland. There are pockets of affluent people, but there are also low-income families struggling to survive, and in rare instances, there is an undercurrent of crime. It is a melting pot filled with many different lifestyles and perspectives of the world. The point is that there's more than meets the eye, and there's rich and insightful experiences on both sides of the track.

Over the years, I attended 10 different schools, and this simultaneously taught me how to be a chameleon. Being a chameleon meant finding ways to make new friends and learning how to fit in. My grandparents, along with my siblings and I, were accepted into a government housing subsidy program which allowed us to move to

Tustin Ranch (near Irvine), an affluent suburb. I went from a more classic-looking high school experience, which was diverse culturally and where everyone came from modest backgrounds to a new school with classmates who were upper-class and had parents who were supportive and involved in their lives. It was a multi-story middle school with an elevator in it.

Because my experience growing up was so different, I felt like a black sheep in my new school. Being the "new girl" meant I received more attention and people were interested in becoming friends, which helped make this transition a lot easier. However, because my new friends had parents who were very involved in their lives, they became innocently curious about where my parents were. I knew they would never understand my upbringing and my experiences, on top of the fact that I didn't know how to explain this to them as a 7th grader. I just wanted to fit in and didn't want to feel alienated.

Out of survival, I began to cultivate my craft as a storyteller. While I didn't want to tell outright lies, I needed to tell a version of the truth that was palatable for them to receive and me to give. Deep down inside, based on their experiences and lack of ability to relate, I knew they would not understand, and I knew that instinctively. Something I've learned as I've gotten older and wiser is that not everyone deserves to know you. Your life is yours, it's a precious part of your soul, and just because you're open and willing to share, doesn't mean that everyone cares or is able to receive it. Your story is a piece of your heart; therefore, you don't give it away to just anyone. There are people who ask questions because they care and want to know, while others just ask questions to be polite or silently judge you. Not everyone deserves to know the full extent of your life's story. I didn't always know or follow this distinction growing up, but I developed a sense of this at this point in my life. "How am I supposed to explain this to my friends?" I thought to myself.

So, the story went something like this: my mom was a nurse (technically true at one point) who lived in Los Angeles (also true) and was planning to move to Tustin Ranch (a hopeful but unlikely dream). I told them my dad lived in Anaheim and kept the rest of the details hazy. Though my story seemed different than the lives of their families, who had stable parents and even more stable incomes, it was at least plausible sounding enough and could explain why my mom was never around. No one would ask further questions but that also meant I could not express my truth. Living in this fractured narrative led me to become comfortable in an additional layer of skin.

I always stood out no matter where I went and learned how to fit in any situation or social circle. My mind and awareness were already more developed and more mature than my classmates. Growing up fast forced me to be more responsible and did not allow me the simple pleasures of being a child.

*

The neighboring houses in Tustin Ranch were large, and we lived in a two-bedroom apartment that was much bigger than our previous home. By the time I was in high school, things had changed—I hated living in Orange County. I felt at home in Los Angeles where my mom was living, where I would visit when my father and her would have a "business transaction." My dad would say, "We're going to visit your mom," but underneath he had multiple intentions—to kill two birds with one stone: let his children see their mom, while also handling his business with his once-wife-turned-business-associate.

I saw this visit as an opportunity to finally tell my mom how I had been feeling about being abandoned, neglected, and the sad fact that my little brother had forgotten what she even looked like. He even requested a photo of my mom from our sister, so that he could remember her. That whole car ride up to LA, I thought about what I was going to say to my mom over and over again. I played the conversation out in my head. I saw myself as brave and strong; I worked up my emotions all the way up to my throat. In Hindu philosophy, the throat chakra is the chakra of communication, or how you express yourself. Each of the chakras represent something different in the body. But the throat chakra is especially important and can be blocked for many reasons, including traumas, sexual abuse, parents telling you to be quiet all the time, or just when people make you feel small and don't listen.

"Hey Mom, can I tell you something?" I asked. But before I uttered a word of my truth, she completely cut me off and said: "Oh, I know, you're going to say that I'm a bad mom. You guys hate me." Everything inside of me that I had worked so hard to say was suddenly stifled and locked away, deep into the back of my throat. I did manage to tell her, however, that my brother forgot what she looked like and requested a photo, hoping that this tidbit of information would give her some sense of how wrong and sad the situation was. But, instead of having any logic or desire to come home with her children, she just said, "Here. I'll give you a photo to give to your sister, so she can give it to your brother." And that's the day that my throat chakra closed.

School is very boring when you have a life like mine. Since I'd had a taste of the real world, and how it flowed, school felt very constricting. With very little effort, I was good at school, received straight As, and was in all honors classes. I was the senior class editor of the yearbook staff and I was voted onto the Homecoming Court and then crowned Winter Formal Queen. But at age 16, I was also partying and drinking since I had a fake ID. I would go out to clubs and bars in West Hollywood any night of the week. I would show up to my teacher's assistant classes in high school wearing a hoodie with sunglasses on, telling the underclassmen about my adventures in Hollywood. As much as I spent my childhood years in Orange County, I consider LA to have raised me.

I had a hotel party in Orange County for my 16th birthday, with my high school friends, who were getting drunk together and having fun, as Orange County high schoolers were prone to do. The following Monday, when I drove to school, I forgot about a half-dozen or so unopened Smirnoff Ice bottles stashed in the trunk of my car. On some random occasions, there were drug dogs who came to school to search students for contraband. The dogs somehow caught the scent of the liquor bottles in my car, and I was suspended. For punishment, I was required to attend AA meetings and enroll in classes about drug and alcohol abuse.

There were two counselors in the classes whom I spent time talking to—relaying my life story—and both were in shock. In hindsight, they asked a highly inappropriate question because it was not only judgmental, but it could have been triggering: "Aren't you scared you are going to become just like your parents?" Had I not been as strong, the question could have impacted me. Undeterred, I responded with conviction: "No. I know I am going to be the opposite of my parents."

By junior year, I was hired by a popular juice bar and later became an assistant manager. In fact, I was the youngest assistant manager they had ever hired. The job gave me the financial means to be more independent. I was able to buy myself nice things, as well as help out my grandparents. My grandmother attempted to help me go after my dreams of being a model, but she was unable to fully execute it as the drive to LA—the time and energy spent transporting me back and forth—was too demanding for her. I always envisioned another life and having this job gave me the ability to have more freedom to explore possibilities beyond my current situation. In the meantime, before I could make that leap on my own, I partied and self-medicated with alcohol on my free time. My free time was most of the time because I managed to do all of my necessary responsibilities—and do them well. I lived the saying: "work hard, play harder."

Innocence Lost

Predator (*noun*): one who injures or exploits others for personal gain or profit.

Like I mentioned before, my grandmother would do anything for anyone, especially for her loved ones. My aunt, my mother's half-sister, frequently relied on my grandmother to help her with everything because she had trouble managing her home life on her own. Although the housing was meant only for my siblings and grandparents, my grandmother bent the rules by allowing my aunt, her husband, and my three cousins to stay with us. That meant 10 people were living in a two-bedroom apartment. If my life had not already been difficult enough, this external pressure and inconvenience, which I had no control over, was now added to my overloaded and stressful situation.

And it was about to take a turn for the worse...

My aunt's husband, whom I identified as my uncle, and I formed a close bond. I trusted him. He was very gregarious and outgoing, and he always seemed to be interested in my well-being. He was basically the "fun uncle." Whenever I'd see him, it was a nice relief and distraction from the undercurrents of all the turmoil around me. This, ladies and gentlemen, is exactly how predators work. First, they gain your trust and make you feel "safe" around them. They are very attentive and create an environment for you to let your guard down. So, when they do attack, it creates a baffling confusion and a deep severing of your innocence.

My siblings and I shared a bedroom. They had bunk beds on one side of the room, and I had my bed on the other. The bathrooms of the apartment were in each room. So, in order to gain access to the bathroom, you needed to enter either my grandparents' room or our room. My aunt and her family slept in the living room and ended up taking over the extra closet in my bedroom (my siblings' closet) as their own. Our bathroom was the communal bathroom for them and guests alike. I never felt like I had my own space, which I didn't, and now the only space that I did have to call my own was about to be invaded.

This living situation turned into a nightmare. I already lacked any feeling of home, structure, foundation and safety—what was left was my trust, which was completely broken one fateful night.

My uncle, who I believed cared for me, and who once upon a time made me feel safe and protected, turned out to be the villain and the perpetrator of this story. Since the bathroom was located in our room, our door had to be left open and available at all times, including all hours of the night. My uncle would come into our room in the middle of the night, pretending to use the restroom, only to approach me, at my most vulnerable time as I slept, and violate me.

*

Molest (verb): to make unwanted or improper sexual advances towards someone, especially to force physical and usually sexual contact on someone.

*

The first night that this happened to me, I slowly began waking up to the most disgusting feeling I'd ever felt. I didn't wake up completely, but when I could see what was going on, I was shocked beyond belief. I was so afraid, sad, confused, embarrassed and I didn't know what to do. In that moment, the first thought I had was to pretend I was really waking up, without letting him know that I was aware of what he was doing, so I moved back and forth as if I was about to wake up, and that's when he backed away and left the room. And, there I was, left alone, in a moment of ultimate betrayal and my innocence lost.

Unfortunately, this would not happen just one time, but on multiple occasions; thankfully only a handful, as in some cases, it can go on for years for other victims. This turned me into an insomniac because I was afraid to go to sleep, fearing that if I fell asleep, he would come in and hurt me again. I could not let that happen. I became savvy and found tactics to avoid this situation, like wrapping myself like a human burrito in a sleeping bag or sleeping with my little sister, but on the inside of the wall, because I knew that it would pose too much of an obstacle. I don't know how long this went on for, but God had answered my prayers and my uncle was arrested—something unrelated to my situation, and as if by a miracle, he was removed from my life. However, the aftermath of his destruction bled into all parts of my life, and became an infected wound until the day I learned how to heal it.

*

You would think after my uncle was arrested, my life would have gotten a lot better, but it didn't. Things only became more complicated as my aunt's chaotic energy seemed to consume the entire apartment. There was no room for me to process the inner turmoil I felt due to my uncle's sexual abuse. Instead, I repressed and self-medicated with alcohol, leaving the house to party and stay with my best friends in order to feel better.

I tried to figure out how to heal on my own. I asked my grandmother if I could see a therapist, which she viewed as something only "for crazy people," which she announced in her little Filipino grandma accent. "You're not crazy," she insisted, "you can talk to me." I scoffed at her idea of therapy—that was exactly the problem. In the nicest way possible, I went out looking for a therapist and eventually found a pro bono counselor in Orange County, who helped me to be heard over the course of a few sessions until his pro bono hours ran out.

Even though I was barely in school, I managed to graduate with excellent grades and enrolled at Orange Coast College. OCC was the path of least resistance. What I was really yearning for was to move to LA. OCC was a playtime version of college for me, with very attractive beach-going students from all over Orange County, and most of my friends were already enrolled. I was not even 18 yet, so school seemed like the logical next step. I took several classes, including "Interpersonal/Intrapersonal Communications" taught by Professor Barbara Bullard, which was the most impactful class I took at OCC that continues to influence me (and probably the only class I went to regularly). The way Professor Bullard taught was unorthodox; she shared higher consciousness material with the students, focusing on learning by going inward and communication through self-awareness.

There were so many moments in Professor Bullard's class that I remember fondly. Through her class, I was attuned to Level One Reiki. Also, as part of the class, we all had an assignment to present our life story to the class. Professor Bullard did not necessarily require everyone to present publicly, as she put it: "If your story is just mom, dad, cat, dog, don't bother—you can just present to your group." This assignment gave me the space to finally tell my story openly and own it, in a way that I had never done before. This was the first time I could tell my truth, and I remember a few people in the class walked away crying. The students in the class were more mature, since people from all walks of life enrolled in community college, including a hairdresser in the class whom I became friends with; after my presentation, she pulled me aside and looked me in the eyes, at age 17, and said, "You have a lot of angels watching over you. Don't forget that."

One day, I walked into Professor Bullard's class and she was about to show a film about quantum physics called *What The Bleep Do We Know?* directed by Mark Vicente. I had never heard of this film before, but it resonated with me, as it discussed themes about collective consciousness and the power of manifestation, which we had gone over that semester. Little did I know, that film would become a lure to joining NXIVM several years later.

Another class I enjoyed at OCC was my acting class. Sometime around then, I became close friends with a girl named "Kitty." Kitty was from Scottsdale, Arizona, and she was an aspiring actress. From that point on, Kitty and I were inseparable. We both wanted to leave Orange County and move to LA. Eventually, we found a cute little apartment in Venice, which basically ended up being an overpriced closet because I would rarely stay there—preferring to let the wind take me wherever I wanted to go around Hollywood. Kitty and I both immersed ourselves in the nightlife, as her uncle was a Hollywood writer and invited us out on the town, which is where I met the nightclub owner I ended up dating.

Once I was in LA, I assimilated quickly and became part of the Hollywood scene. I was fully immersed in the lifestyle everyone in Hollywood, at some point or another, seems to fall into. There I found what I was looking for: risk, call to adventure, celebrities—but there was also repression, trauma, and self-medicating with parties and boys. This period of time was the opposite of the search I later found myself on through NXVIM.

At that time, Hollywood was all about having fun, devoid of social media and influencers. Parties were silly, loud and raucous, which made everything seem like a playground. One night I was working at a fabled Hollywood hot spot, and then the next day I was flying on a private jet to Aspen to stay in the Presidential Suite (this was not a "tag your sponsor" situation). On many nights of the week, I would go out with my friends to our usual haunts, never waiting in line (walking in with the owners), then ending up in the Hills at some of the most fabulous after-parties overlooking all of LA. This was just a regular Tuesday for me.

Beyond the glitz and glamour, there was a dark underbelly to the Hollywood scene that I became familiar with. Those poor souls in nightlife were seeking repair, in part because they were entirely consumed by the need for external validation and also mistook the lack of depth in Hollywood for something actually meaningful. They had no idea who they really were outside their own façade. Drug abuse, recklessness, and insecurities were all frequent occurrences, along with general self-absorption that comes with immaturity. Many who had tons of money were also damaged, flaunting around their cash like a flamingo in a zoo to hide the fact that, if they did not have money, they would be the thing they feared most: mediocre.

The moment-to-moment pain was internal, which is why I masked it with partying, alcohol, and running away from my family. It was too much to bear. I couldn't deal with my reality, so I indulged in the new reality I was part of. The thread started to unwind at the seams. I thought I was happy, but in my time alone, I knew there was something nagging at my heart. Something wasn't right. This became abundantly clear after having a heart-to-heart with one of my friends, and for the first time in a long time, I talked about my mother. As soon as the word "mom" left my lips, my stomach gurgled, and I immediately ran to the bathroom to purge—clearly, I was carrying something that had been festering underneath the surface, which was ready to be seen. Shortly after that awareness occurred, it was my "21st birthday," but I was actually turning 20 (technically, I turned 21 many times over).

All I wanted to do for my birthday was to sing karaoke with my friends at my favorite spot. My dad and I had a good relationship, and I wanted to invite him along with his girlfriend, to help me celebrate. When I showed my friends the dress I was going to wear, which was a low-cut, backless dress, they asked, "You're going to wear that *even though* your dad is coming?" I replied, "Yes, nobody cares about what I do." That is truly how I felt deep down inside—that no one cared about me, and therefore didn't care about what I chose to do.

Boy, was I wrong. My dad arrived later to the party, where I was already drunk and in my dress. As soon as he walked in, he was red-faced with anger, shouting, "Who do you think you are? Mariah Carey or something?" He was fuming, but I was drunk and dealing with my underage, fake id-less friends trying to get into the bar. Eventually, we left the bar altogether. My "normal" birthday tradition was to puke, blackout, and forget about everything, and this year was not going to be any different—I would not be deterred by my dad or anyone else. Until the next morning, when I had an epiphany. That morning was a final moment of realization, where I felt that I would no longer be desperate. I realized the only reason I was dressing that way was to receive the attention I was lacking from my parents and that, in reality, I did not need to do this anymore. I wanted to leave this cycle, so something had to give.

After my birthday, I decided to go inwards. I traded the life I had drinking booze to taking down heart-opening tonics at the Erewhon in

West Hollywood. This grocery store was a friendly place where all the staff and patrons seemed to be brimming with knowledge of health and wellness. It was a place of elevated well-being and consciousness; people were friendly, peaceful, and astonishingly open and vulnerable about their emotions. I became vegan and started to heal myself, particularly focusing on detoxing, yoga, and colonics. I even worked at a vegan restaurant for the next year and a half, which was a huge part of me delving into my new path of self-awareness and self-realization.

The Call

A friend of mine was a bodyworker; I was very close with her, and she allowed me to be in a vulnerable state. When she massaged me, she started to karate chop my back, which triggered an overwhelming sensation of energy. It was as if I began to panic and hyperventilate. She somehow understood there was deep trauma being held in my body. Soon she was asking me firmly, "Tell me what happened. Tell me what happened." Shaking with tears streaming down my face, I told her that my uncle had molested me. We went to look at this trauma together, which was, up until that point, a secret. It was the first time I had spoken up about the molestation in a very long time. This was the first time I could remember hearing myself speak about it since my therapy session in Orange County.

How many years would go by until I finally confronted my uncle? At that time, I was in the market for an acting manager, and a friend of mine referred me to a well-known manager (who was incidentally equally well-known for being a prick). During the meeting, he gave me three sets of "sides" or lines for commercials and television and told me to read them. It was a "frozen" read, meaning I did not have any time to prepare.

There was so much anxiety, fear, and stress coursing through my body. It was more than just stage fright; after all, I was comfortable in front of audiences. Long story short, I blew the audition and came to a realization: I would not be successful if I did not confront the sexual abuse trauma I had experienced earlier on in my life. In other words, the abuse was hindering my creativity, and the only way to overcome this was to deal with it directly.

I decided to go to the source and confront my uncle.

*

After my uncle had been released from prison, I heard through the grapevine that he and my aunt were in communication again. I decided to enlist the help of my sister, in order to find a way to see him and have the opportunity to confront him once and for all. My aunt and I had not spoken for a couple of years, though my sister had been closer to her and arranged for me to meet so the three of us could get together and I could share my story. Initially, my aunt was shocked, confused and upset—she did not want to believe that her ex-husband had done the worst thing imaginable, and to her niece, no less. But the further I went into detail and exposed the layers of trauma that had taken so long for me to gather the courage to bring to the surface, the more she knew that I was telling the truth.

My aunt arranged to meet with my uncle at a local gas station where the plan was to surprise him when he least expected it. As we pulled into the lot, I sat in the backseat with my aunt's new baby and stared into the rearview mirror until I saw his car pull up. My uncle stepped out and waved at my aunt, who walked over briskly to talk to him while I readied myself to get out of the car. Suddenly, I put my hand on the door handle and felt the anxiety building. "It's now or never," I told myself, as the door swung open and I jolted across the parking lot towards my uncle, who looked like he had just seen a ghost.

"You and I need to have a conversation about something," I stammered. He looked confused on the surface, but I could tell he was scared. "What do you mean?" he replied. I was ready to breathe fire. "Do you remember what happened when you were living with us at the apartment?" I paused. "No," he said, playing dumb, "I don't know what you're talking about. Did something happen to you?" he asked. "Do I need to walk you through exactly what happened?" I pleaded, as I had no choice but to go through the excruciating details with him. I proceeded to explain what he had done to me, and how he ruined the trust I had in both him and men in general. I was utterly fucked up, and all he could say in response, in addition to denying anything happened, was, "I obviously did something to you, I mean, something must've happened because you're clearly upset," he trailed off.

By this point, steaming hot tears of rage were pouring down my face. Why would I make this up? "Did something like this ever happen to you?" I asked, referring to the abuse. He scoffed. At that point, I could tell he would never take any responsibility for what he had done. By the end, I knew there was only one thing left to say: "You're going to have to live with this for the rest of your life. It's on you now, not me." I looked at my aunt and sister, both of whom had fixated on my uncle. "Let's go," I commanded. "I'm finished here."

Within my journey, I was focused singularly on my healing and well-being. However, I was still in LA and still needed to make money. My friend gave me an opportunity to work at a hot new nightclub in West Hollywood, so I eventually ended up returning to the Hollywood scene, this time working as a bottle service girl. This environment and lifestyle was already very familiar to me, as well as being very lucrative. So lucrative, in fact, that I would walk out of the club on a slow night with a fistful of cash. On a big night, I would take home upwards of a thousand dollars or more. Money was plentiful and I only needed to work three days a week to fuel my expensive wellness routine. I was not your average bottle service girl—I was fresh off of a yoga retreat in India with two Vipassanas (ten-day silent meditation retreat) under my belt. So, instead of upselling more champagne, I ended up sitting with the clients at their table to discuss the Universe and what they really wanted in life, rather than wasting money on feeding their ego. That's all a nightclub is anyway—an arena of unsatiated egos.

I was on my path to healing and wellness, but that did not mean that I completely dispelled my shadows. It was easy to fall back into the nightlife scene, in a far less problematic way, but the reality was that I was stepping back to the complacent days where my soul was dying. With my bottle service job, I was trapped in golden handcuffs—alive but not really living.

My best friend at the time, Gabriella, who was also interested in personal development, told me about a new course that some of her clients were coaches in. Gabriella was working in multi-level marketing with some success, having won a Lexus for selling anti-aging face cream, but she also worked as a colon hydro therapist, where she met most of her clients in the course. Gabriella was planning to host a barbecue at her place in West Hollywood, which is where I met India Oxenberg for the first time.

India seemed nice and sweet, and at the barbecue she invited me to a presentation she was giving about "Executive Success Programs" or "ESP" the following week at Gabriella's. I later learned that India's mother, Catherine, was a star in the TV show *Dynasty*, and that her grandmother was the Princess of Yugoslavia. But despite these fanciful things, India seemed humble, and she made me interested in checking out her informal presentation about ESP. I told her I would drop by.

The next week, I arrived again at Gabriella's place around 4 o'clock. It was near the end of spring and the sun was still shining, so this time we sat in the courtyard, where the patio furniture was arranged around a giant white paper flip pad on a stand. There were three coaches there: India, Michel, and Mark, who was a "Proctor." Michel led the presentation, starting off by asking a question, "Think about what it is that you want most in life." People in the crowd were engaged. "Is it a house? A car? A certain lifestyle? What about six-pack abs?" There were chuckles. He said, "Imagine you want a six-pack," and he began drawing on the board. "You start telling yourself, I want a six-pack, and you believe you can have it, so you start off taking the first steps." He progressed the pen further on the white paper board. "OK, so you start dieting," he made another mark on the board, "and then you start going to the gym. You slowly start seeing results, so you go to the gym again and again." He paused to make more marks.

"But then something happens." He scribbled a strike on the board, indicating a separation. "You get tired and decide you don't want to go to the gym. Then, the next day, it's a friend's birthday and you want to eat cake. Sooner or later," he then drew a more pronounced mark, "you no longer are remotely close to a six-pack. This is what we call your inner deficiencies, or your own limitations that hold you back in life from achieving your goals." By this point, Michel had worked the crowd into a frenzy. "With our patent-pending technology, we can help you remove these inner deficiencies, allowing you to reach your highest human potential." So many things were going through my mind—part of it sounded too good to be true, and another part of it sounded like this could be the answer.

Michel concluded his presentation with a question: "Do you want to reach your highest human potential?" and then introduced Mark and India, who were going to share their testimonials. I'm not easily impressed by things of a self-help nature that promise to change your life, since I had many experiences in this arena. India told us about her experience with ESP over the past several years, and she detailed the many ways that it had impacted her positively through her experience in the organization. Hers was a nice story, but I was not impressed. However, Mark Vicente was a name I had heard before, and when he told us he directed and produced *What The Bleep Do We Know?* I immediately recalled seeing his film in Professor Bullard's class at OCC. Now I was listening. Mark's film gave him clout, which enabled me to take his testimonial seriously.

The price of the course was expensive—a little over $3,000 for the first five days of a 16-day intensive. I decided to fill out an application and put down a $500 deposit on the spot. I went home excited and immediately told my boyfriend at the time, Tej, that I had applied to take this $3,000 -plus course and couldn't wait until it started. Without him wanting to burst my bubble, as he saw how happy I was, Tej also felt the need to give me his honest opinion. He was concerned that I was falling for a "scheme," as he explained, "If they were really trying to help people, it shouldn't cost *this much*. This is a lot of money—what do you really know about this course? Something doesn't feel right." I tried not to be completely deflated, but his words of care and caution did prompt me to do some deeper digging.

On the first couple pages of Google, there were articles coming up about ESP and the umbrella organization it fell under called "NXIVM." Some of these articles discussed NXIVM being a "scam," a "cult," and many more comments with negatively charged details about the organization. But on the same page of Google, there were pictures of the Dalai Lama putting a ceremonial sash around the neck of NXIVM's founder, a man named Keith Raniere, also known as "Vanguard." Although there were some positive images associated with NXIVM, I was turned off completely by the negative articles, and I texted India to ask that she withdraw my application and relinquish the deposit I had just submitted. That's when India messaged back, asking if everything was O.K. I told her I had found a lot of weird stuff online about NXIVM.

India asked if she could call me to talk on the phone. When I answered, she was very calm and collected: "I totally understand how you're feeling right now," she said, "and I felt the same way. We've actually been trying to get those articles off the internet for a while now. But the people who put those up are *very powerful* and have a lot of money." She paused, then began the story: "There was a son of a giant media mogul; his family owned a bunch of news outlets. He took ESP, but then realized his family business was unethical and really corrupt. He told his family he wanted no part of it, which upset his parents. His parents created a smear campaign against Keith and NXIVM." This story seemed plausible and addressed some of the concerns I had. India continued: "You can totally get your deposit back, but I'm not in charge of it—I'll talk to Mark and have him reach out to you."

The next day, Mark sent me a text message asking if I was free to chat. I picked up the phone when he called and told him that I wanted to withdraw my application and get my money back. Mark was also very calm and equally understanding: "I have no problem giving your deposit back to you," he said, "but I am just curious—why the change of heart?" I told him, "I've been saving this money to go back to Hawaii, and I just don't know if this course is worth it." There was a pause on the phone. Mark took a breath in. "I totally understand," he said, "Hawaii is nice. Sure, you can go there and have a great time. But you know *that* feeling? *That* feeling will still be there when you come back." Inside, I asked myself: "How did he know *that* feeling deep down inside that was gnawing at me and chewing at my subconscious?"

Mark then said: "This is an opportunity for you to get rid of *that* feeling. So, how about this? If you take ESP, and you're not happy with it, we'll give you your money back. Out of all the people who have ever taken ESP, there's only been one person who ever asked for their money back, and we gave it to them." With Mark's reassuring words, all my concerns about wasting my money went out the window. "What's the worst that can happen?" I thought to myself, "Spend a few thousand dollars and lose a few days of my life? But what if this is something that can really help me?" I got quiet and tapped in to my inner-self, and asked it if I should enroll in ESP. I heard an answer back: "Yes." Then I told Mark, "O.K., fine. I'm in."

*

It was August 2016. Gabriella, myself, and Gabriella's friend Robin went to the first day of the ESP orientation in LA. The orientation was in a rental studio space, usually used for castings. The inside was an open floor plan made from grey cement cinderblock, glossy concrete flooring, with white walls and wood finishing, as well as some California sunlight pouring through. This was the day before the course began, when everyone participating would be meeting each other for the first time. For a couple hours, we learned the rules and guidelines: the only food we could eat was vegetarian, we learned our schedule, and received our binders. It felt like orientation for the first day of school—I was excited and giddy, looking forward to diving in.

There was about thirty of us. A hodge-podge of people from all walks of life—a millionaire CEO, Harvard graduates, people in the entertainment industry, and even a 12-year-old boy with Tourette's syndrome. This 12-year-old was on his fourth round of ESP. His mother praised the ESP coursework as it had rid her son of his ticks. Upon hearing about his recovery, it was astonishing to think that something like this could help cure someone of their Tourette's syndrome. Seeing this kid in person, I would have never guessed he had Tourette's—it was the proof in the pudding that ESP worked.

The course started at eight in the morning and sometimes went until nine in the evening. There were several Proctors from NXIVM there, including Mark Hildreth and Jim Del Negro, who looked like the classic sitcom dad, tall and super loving to everyone. There were also coaches there, including India, helping to facilitate. We were also introduced to Nancy Salzman, who held the title of "Prefect," and was the CEO of NXIVM. Nancy appeared on a taped video recording that felt like a 1980's infomercial—big hair, makeup, corny graphics, and probably on VHS. It was astonishing that we paid alot of money to watch those videos, as they were clearly out of date and had low production quality. It made me wonder where the money actually went.

We were instructed to wear our sashes, which were white like a karate belt, signaling that we were beginners in ESP. As a larger group, we watched videos diving into the curriculum and were asked to think critically about broad questions, such as "What is freedom?" or "What is law?" These were thought-provoking questions that people were not generally accustomed to debating out loud.

We also learned about "neuro-linguistic programming" from Nancy, which is a tool taught by people like Tony Robbins, often to help people who are working in sales get better results. The gist of NLP was about how people take in information; some people, for example, are activated by money, others by altruism, and if you can read their typology, you can understand more about how to connect with people. It's a great tool for training salespeople since every potential customer is different and learning why a certain pitch appeals to that person can ultimately make it easier to sell to them.

The reason we were being taught NLP was to show us things that most people don't know, such as a greater awareness of how others operate, be it emotionally, verbally or in their thought process. Because NLP was not universally known, it made us feel that we had a secret, or a key, that few else had—it separated us from the rest of the world and made us better than them. Looking back now, it also makes sense why they taught us NLP, as recruiting people became a huge part of the structure, and it gave us a leg-up above the rest.

After we broke out of the big group, we had a lunch break and then moved into our smaller groups. In the smaller groups, we heard each other's stories, which allowed us to become open and vulnerable with complete strangers. It was fascinating to hear about people's wildest dreams, their shame, and their humility in a safe space. This experience was beautiful, as the group became closer to each other, like a family. A continued experience of the process went deeper over the course of the next five days. I got to a certain place within myself where I felt totally empowered, able to identify my limitations and where I learned tools to overcome these limitations. I was on a high, in complete joy and bliss— and I wanted more.

On the last day, they showed us clips of the other curriculums available in NXIVM, such as "The Source," which was for artists and performers, or "V-Week," which was an adult summer camp celebration of Keith Raniere's birthday with like-minded individuals (it looked like utopia). If you signed up for the "Middle Five" of the 16-day course on the last day, you could get a discount—it was just shy of $4,000. NXIVM had courses all over the world, including in Albany, where Keith and many of the higher-ups in NXIVM lived. I was very curious and wanted to take my next course in Albany, so I signed up.

Since August 2016, it felt like I put my foot on the gas pedal and never took it off. It was as if all of a sudden there had been an uptick in blessings, or a shift in my life that poured in positivity. Money was coming in because I was booking photoshoots and other jobs. My sister and Tej planned a surprise birthday party for me, which was one of the best birthdays I'd ever had. Everything seemed to be going amazingly well for the first time in a long time. In addition, the new friends I was making all felt like part of my new purpose, in contrast to the more superficial friendships I had cultivated before I took ESP. My hunger to grow and keep learning about myself was almost insatiable.

In 2016 Gabriella and I flew into New York City and then rode the Chinatown bus up to Albany. On the bus, we made friends with another person who was also going to NXIVM—we could tell just by looking at him that he was headed there as well. When we finally arrived in Albany, it was late in the evening. India picked us up from the bus station and the first place she took us to was to "volleyball" at the Sports Barn in Albany.

Albany is a small town, and late at night it was pitch black, except for the few streetlights that dotted the landscape. A thin layer of fresh snow coated everything. The air was cold and crisp, which felt nice, and invigorating, being there for the first time. It felt like a new land of adventure. India picked us up from the bus station in a black BMW, which we later found out belonged to Alison Mack. Gabriella, myself, and Sam (our new friend we met on the bus), hopped into the car and India whisked us away to the Sports Barn. When we parked, Gabriella stayed on the phone talking to her boyfriend in the car. I noticed India's bright eyes light up when she told me that I would be meeting Keith for the first time. She was elated, and so was I.

At half past eleven in the evening, I walked into the Sports Barn where Keith and a bunch of NXIVM people were playing their last set of volleyball. Like the videos of Nancy Salzman, the gym was old, sunburnt, with a feeling of 1980s nostalgia. After the game wrapped up, Keith sat down in a chair near the court and started to put things away in his duffle bag. India beckoned me to come over so that I could be introduced to Keith.

When I set my eyes on Keith, I was underwhelmed—he did not seem like anything amazing, not just in terms of his looks, but he seemed to have no aura whatsoever. Nevertheless, because I had such a life-changing experience in ESP, I felt an immense amount of gratitude for Keith because he created the course that had impacted me greatly. I felt that Keith had the same goal as me, which was to change the world. It made me overwhelmed with emotion, so much so that I began to cry, as I was projecting my experience in ESP, and my belief in him, onto him. I felt so close to him because he was the brainchild of ESP, which I loved so dearly. After I had my big, emotional breakdown, Keith gently grabbed my hand and walked me over to the bench. He looked deep into my eyes and asked me why I was crying, which I responded with, "I'm just so emotional and grateful." Keith looked at me and said, "I'm glad that you're here." That concluded the night.

The very next morning was the first day of the Middle Five of the course. Jim Del Negro was again serving as the head trainer, and there was around the same number of attendees as the first five days in LA, except now the people in attendance were from places much farther away. There was a pop star from the U.K., a sailor from Italy, a few people from affluent families in Mexico, and then other people like me, around my age.

Before I saw the "Albany Center," I assumed it would have been a grand building with all the trappings of a well-endowed organization. But, in reality, the Albany Center was a suite in a non-descript commercial building that would have ordinarily been lined with rows of cubicles. There was a kitchen, multiple rooms, meeting spaces and a framed photo of Keith and Nancy. The building felt sanitized, like a shell of a place, the kind of building where people would rent out space to teach you how to sell life insurance. This was surprising given the cost of the coursework, but I didn't mind because I was excited to do the work.

The Middle Five was similar to the first five days but with different modules. There was a module all about "secrets," which involved disclosing embarrassing things about ourselves. The idea was that if we shared our secrets, no matter how embarrassing or scary, it would relieve us of the burden. The environment felt like a safe space, reinforced by the fact that we all signed non-disclosure agreements before we began. Other than the different modules, everything else was the same—we had lunch breaks, snacks, broke into small groups and watched similarly outdated videos of Nancy Salzman taking us through the curriculum.

*

Before I arrived in Albany, India and I had become close friends. After the first "Five Day", I felt open, raw and vulnerable; India made herself available to help me process the experience I had, and I really began to trust her. India had also recently relocated to Albany. Because India and I were close, she wanted to talk to me about something she thought I would be interested in. So, on a lunch break, India asked me to go on a walk with her so she could tell me all about it.

On the walk, India told me about this "thing" she wanted to invite me into, which she said had helped her tremendously. India had been in it for only a year, but the experience had been more impactful than the entirety of her seven years in NXIVM. I loved ESP so much, I couldn't imagine that there was something *even better* out there. India explained that this "thing" was a secret group, full of high-powered women. It seemed like a bad-ass women's bootcamp—basically, a women's-only mentorship program to help women become even more powerful. But, in order to learn more about it, I would have to hand over three pieces of collateral to protect the privacy of the group: family, finances, and reputation. This was a prerequisite for anyone who wanted to find out more about the group—even before being invited in formally as a member.

"We don't invite just anyone into it," India said, explaining that the collateral served as protection for people who came from lofty, elite backgrounds. Indeed, India herself was the daughter of a famous actress and the granddaughter of the former Princess of Yugoslavia—if anyone had something to lose, she would. India's collateral consisted of financial information, a family heirloom and a secret. As an unassuming blonde wallflower, India completely disarmed any feeling of fear I had towards this members-only group. It also seemed like the invitation from India to join was an answer to my prayers—the opportunity to learn from a group of women devoted to being the best versions of themselves in order to ultimately help humanity. But not only that, India told me that the group was only open to certain women—women who wanted to push their boundaries and limitations and, as a result, had an unconventional approach that needed to be kept secret.

After my walk with India, I started to compile my three pieces of collateral that I would need to give her to learn more about the group. I gave India two secrets and a notarized document. It felt weighted, but I knew the whole purpose of the collateral was to protect the group. It also felt exciting, as I was about to learn so much more information in ESP, but also combine what I would be taught in the women's group. I had no intention of stopping as I wanted to continue to elevate. After I submitted my collateral, India met me on a walk to tell me that I had been accepted as a member, and she said that she would be serving as my mentor. India told me that, upon meeting me, she had already wanted to invite me into this group, as she saw my potential to learn and grow from the experience, just as she had.

I returned to the Middle Five brimming with excitement, only to realize that the week was coming to an end. After the Middle Five, there was the Final Six days of the course left, but I did not have the means to do it. I became very sad, knowing that I would have to leave soon and come back later to finish. One day, I went to volleyball and saw Keith there. It was very rare to find Keith, except at volleyball, and even more rare to be invited to speak to him one-on-one. Keith asked me how I was enjoying the course, and he kept telling me that it was good that I had come to Albany. It felt bittersweet to hear him say that, as I informed him that I would be leaving soon. "But you could just stay," he remarked in a dry tone of voice. "Yeah," I said, "but I just paid for the Middle Five and I'll take the final days of the course later." Keith was unphased, instead insisting again: "But you could just stay." The entire conversation started to annoy me. "Yeah, I would stay if this course wasn't so expensive," I thought to myself. But Keith continued to insist. "I have to go back to work, in order to pay for the next six days of the course," I told him, but he did not relent. I looked at him puzzled. "I understand people have jobs, obligations, or things of that nature," then he looked at me and delivered a bomb: "but are you the master of your life, or is your life the master of you?"

Upon hearing this question, I felt an ignition go off inside of me—as if I had solved the puzzle or finally realized the missing component of the equation that had stumped me for years. The question blew my mind, and the more I thought about it, the more I realized that I was not content to just go back home. "Go back to what?" I thought, "My deteriorating relationship? The apartment I'm living in? My job?" None of it seemed appealing to me, compared to the possibility of staying in Albany and finishing the course. I didn't want to leave. At that moment, I decided I was going to stay and make it work, to finish the remaining six days, any way I could.

After my conversation with Keith, I went to dinner with a friend, Jenna, who was living at Allison Mack's house at 7 General's Way. Jenna was one of the people I related to the most—she was vibrant, full of spunk, and deeply empathetic—like your favorite camp counselor. At dinner, I explained to Jenna what Keith had said—about how he insisted I should stay, but that I was not able to do it without some help. "You could ask about a payment plan," Jenna said, "or if not, I'll just loan you the money." There, after a single conversation, my problem was solved. The next day, I went to ask about a payment plan, but I was told that there was no option available then, so I went into my rolodex and called on a favor from a friend who once offered to loan me money if I ever needed it. A few hours later, the money was wired over, and I was set to finish the course in Albany. A limitation was conquered and overcome, and I was doing exactly what I wanted to do, as the "master of my life."

The second part of the course began with "Emotion of Meaning" or "EMs." To showcase the EMs, they brought in a special guest, none other than the infamous Prefect, Nancy Salzman, live and in the flesh, who performed a demonstration. Nancy was one of the higher-ups in NXIVM, so being with her was a special treat. Nancy asked if there were any volunteers who wanted to go through an EM. A woman raised her hand and invited her to the stage, and asked her what she wanted to get rid of. The woman explained that she was deathly afraid of bees. In fact, even the thought of bees would cause her to break out into hives—she was so afraid of bees that she started to cry even before the EM began. Bees made her feel like she was going to die.

Nancy took her through the EM, asking questions about her childhood and coaxing out powerful memories. As Nancy prodded, the woman began to explain that she had been greatly embarrassed by something that had happened in her childhood—which had to do with bees. Through the series of questions in the EM process, it was revealed that her fear of bees was not a fear at all: it was a trigger from childhood that made her fear extreme embarrassment, which was projected onto the bees. Once this memory had been unearthed, Nancy explained that there was now a bee in the room, buzzing around her head, perhaps coming close enough to sting her. Within a matter of minutes, the woman who was deathly afraid of bees and would break out into hives just thinking about them a moment ago, was no longer reactive—her fear had dissipated completely. My EMs entailed a similar process, focusing on childhood trauma and abandonment I experienced as a child.

As told, ESP was a grueling process, which was not fun. It forced you to look directly at the ugliest parts of yourself. However, we were constantly being told to "wait for the 'Magnificent Series.'" The Magnificent Series was the last three days of the course when we would switch perspectives, to relish in all the good things about ourselves, and to see what we really stood for. Allison Mack was the Proctor for my Magnificent Series. When I first met her, she appeared to be kind, empathetic, and self-assured. She also seemed to be very attentive, asked a lot of questions, and seemed particularly interested in me as a person.

Towards the end, I had been making up different sayings and catch-phrases using "ESPian" terms. I would share my little slogans with people in my group, and eventually some of the material I had come up with got around. Jim and some of the NXIVM higher-ups heard through the grapevine about these sayings, and eventually suggested I do *something* with them—like put them on a bumper sticker or on a t-shirt. Jim told me that Keith had actually owned a t-shirt company, and that I should talk to him about collaborating. What started as an off-the-cuff joke was slowly turning into something bigger—like a humanitarian t-shirt company. I had some prior knowledge about the t-shirt business (from an ex-boyfriend), but with the help of Keith and the support of people around me, I thought that maybe we could do something.

I was again offered a discounted special to take another course by the end of Day Sixteen. They gave a list of all the courses they offered, and suggested I take advantage of the early-bird discount. I was very interested in "The Source," but the price was steep: $11,000 for 11 days in Vancouver, which did not include food, lodging, or transportation. "The Source" was a company founded by Allison Mack and Keith for artists, actors, and performers to reach their highest potential in creativity and mastering their craft. I told India I was interested in The Source, but it was outside my budget; she suggested I talk to Allison—maybe there was a payment plan available, or a "work-trade."

Later, India and I went on another walk so that she could unveil a new detail about this women's group I had just joined. The group had two names, but I was privy to only one of them: it was called "The Vow." India went on to explain that in The Vow, there were boundaries being pushed around language, especially in using terms to address India as my mentor. As she explained, it is no different than a "master" and "sensei" in karate, or a "guru" in yoga, and other things of that nature. The Vow also used names. She said the names were meant to make us feel uncomfortable and stir up feelings. "You're going to refer to me as 'master,' and you will be my 'slave.'" The way India said this, was as if those words had no meaning—they were just words, not a very big deal. She prefaced that The Vow was very unconventional in it's teachings and was created for the members to push against their boundaries of limitation. Once again, coming from India, it was easy to overlook details, even though this was the beginning of a long journey of indoctrination.

After I completed the ESP course, we all joined up together to celebrate the experience we had just gone through. They threw us a party in the woods, with a bonfire and ice cream. It was so cold outside that the ice cream didn't even need to be put into a cooler, but it stayed cold in the chilly Albany evening. Looking up at the night sky, there was no light pollution, and it was one of the first times I could see the stars so brightly. It felt so surreal to be eating ice cream in the woods in Albany with these people that I loved—everything seemed perfect.

I had a couple of days left in Albany before I was supposed to head back to LA. In those remaining days, I had two goals in mind: first, to talk to Allison Mack about enrolling in The Source, and secondly, to walk with Keith to talk about the t-shirt company. India arranged a meeting with Allison at her apartment, which was down the street from the house she owned on 7 General's Way in Clifton Park, and was where she lived. Allison's apartment was cozy, quaint, and decorated with lots of trinkets—it had a nice, home-y feeling.

When I arrived at Allison's house, she let me get settled and we sat down to chat. "So, what did you want to talk about?" she asked. I told her I really wanted to take The Source, but it was too expensive, and I wanted to ask if I could set up a payment plan. I was so nervous to ask for help, but I let out a sigh of relief when I did it—I was glad that I had gotten this off of my chest. If she said no, at last I had tried. "You recently learned that India is your Master, right?" My eyes widened. "Well, I am India's Master. Which means that I am your 'Grandmaster.'" I felt shocked as she continued: "Since I'm your Grandmaster, you'll be able to take The Source and have a lot of other privileges. If you enroll three other people to take the class, yours will be covered." I had already put a $3,000 deposit down, but never mind that, I would be able to enroll people to take the class for free—"and if you don't enroll people, you can work it off," she said.

I was so excited to take the course, but equally excited to learn that Allison was my Grandmaster. Allison was a successful actress who had starred in a hit TV show, *Smallville*. There was a lot that I could learn from her. Feeling giddy, I had accomplished my first goal within the few days I had remaining. Next, I went to go track down Keith, most likely at volleyball, and talk to him about the t-shirt company. At a break during the game, I approached Keith and pitched him the idea. He told me to get his contact information from Allison so that we could discuss it further.

On my very last night in Albany, Allison gave me Keith's contact information and I sent him a message via What's App to ask if he was around for a walk. He made no promises, but he said he would try to make something happen, although he was very busy. He messaged me to ask if I could go on a walk with him later on in the night, which I had no problem with. People said that walking with Keith was special and that it did not happen often, but if you were fortunate to walk with him, it would change your life. As soon as other people in the community heard I had been invited to walk with Keith, I noticed them looking at me with side-eyes. On one hand, I felt special because I was being singled out to meet with Keith; on the other hand, I genuinely felt that I had an idea that could benefit NXIVM.

The text messages from Keith were getting later and later, and I kept my phone near me throughout the night waiting, until finally it was two in the morning, and he was available. I found Keith outside and we started to walk around Clifton Park. It was pitch black out, and there was very little light except for the reflection of the streetlights on the snowbanks plowed on the edge of the sidewalk. Walking with Keith brought up a lot of feelings, although at the same time, I didn't really know what to feel.

I was getting what I wanted: to start a business and forge a mentor-mentee relationship with Keith. However, I also felt strange because Keith was a person who apparently had an unusually high-I.Q., was "one of the world's greatest humanitarians," and was an overall exceptional person—I just was not entirely sure what we would be discussing. "You can ask me anything you want," he said. I asked questions to get to know him, about his home life, and then eventually we started to talk about the t-shirt company. I explained that I had helped an ex-boyfriend start a t-shirt company in the past and that I was somewhat well-versed in the business, but more importantly, I had some great ideas. As it turned out, Keith did own a t-shirt company with a screen-printing studio in Mexico, which was affiliated with a well-known fashion company. Even more coincidentally, Keith had been looking for the right person to run the business. By the end of the walk, he requested that I formulate a business plan and send it to him, outlining what I envisioned.

I returned to LA filled with excitement about my experience, as well as the feeling of unlimited possibilities. My soul, once dying, was on fire. I was beaming with energy and diving into things that really mattered to me. I kept booking gigs, going to castings, and working at the nightclub, but I was also gearing up to take The Source in Vancouver, which was only a month away in December. I had never been to Vancouver before.

Vancouver was a clean city, full of nice people, and it felt very welcoming. Robin had already signed up for The Source, and since we were going to be together in Vancouver, I helped arrange to stay with another friend I met through NXIVM named Stephanie. I met Stephanie during my Eleven Day—she and I bonded instantly and felt like kindred spirits. To this day, she is one of my closest friends. Stephanie was a jewelry maker and a body worker living in Vancouver, who graciously opened her home to both me and Robin (whom she had never met before). The course was taking place at the Vancouver Center, which was owned by Sarah Edmondson, an actress and a high-level proctor in NXIVM. I was ready for a deep dive into The Source and set out to do more work.

Allison and another Proctor, Mark Hildreth, who was also an actor, would be leading the course. Mark and I had become acquainted at my Five Day beforehand, and I felt grateful that he would be there to lead The Source. Mark was a very kind, sweet man and a great example of what a man could be—he was open-hearted but firm in his masculinity.

Before I got to Vancouver, India gave me a new assignment to start thinking about other women I thought would be interested in joining The Vow. Women who were strong, courageous, and wanted to improve themselves. Women I thought would benefit from The Vow. After spending time with Robin in Vancouver during The Source, I thought she might be interested as she admitted that one of her fears was that she lacked deep female friendships and desperately wanted to change that. Allison and I became close during The Source, and it was fun because we both shared a little secret. The work in The Source was deep and impactful, as well as emotionally exhausting. Every day there were multiple massive breakthroughs. I felt a deeper sense of self and a stronger knowingness of who I truly am.

Around the middle of The Source, Allison took me aside from the group to tell me that she loved Robin and really wanted her to be in The Vow. Now, although I did consider Robin would want to join, especially because she was obsessed with Allison (a big fan girl), I personally didn't feel ready—or have the desire to take on another responsibility, especially because I just joined and didn't even know what I was doing in The Vow. I wanted to get good at this thing before inviting anyone else, let alone overseeing them.

Thus far, The Vow felt less like a sorority and more like being deserted on an island, because the only communication about The Vow—outside of my Grandmaster Allison—was with India. There was no interaction otherwise, and I had very little idea about what I was even really doing, but I was still being asked to recruit for it. Initially, the only things that I was doing was sending India a "GM" and "GN" on Telegram, an encrypted messaging platform, to say good morning and good night. However, I did begin asking Robin certain questions to see if The Vow was something she would be interested in—without fully giving anything away. And she seemed like a prime candidate. She wanted to grow, wanted certain things out of life, and answered questions that fit with the profile of a woman who belonged in The Vow. We ended up spending Christmas in Vancouver together, and even got snowed-in one of the days. Robin and I began to become very close.

On Christmas Eve, the Vancouver Center threw a party. Meanwhile, Allison kept pressuring me to invite Robin into "The Vow," against my better judgment. Allison was with me when I began to start the process of recruiting Robin. I did such a poor job that Allison cut me off in the very beginning and recruited Robin herself. I said, "See, there's this thing—it's a women's-only group. . . for empowerment . . ." I trailed off. Allison jumped in. I couldn't sell something that I didn't even really know about—basically, all I could do was just parrot what India and Allison had told me about The Vow. Allison said, "We're part of this special group of women," and continued to explain that she loved Robin and wanted her to join The Vow. Before Robin knew anything else about The Vow, she agreed to join, and we ended up on FaceTime with India once Robin said "yes." It was like a happy little family had formed.

Allison then gave Robin the instructions to come up with the three pieces of collateral to complete the process. Both Allison and Robin were very desperate. They were going through the enrollment process at warp speed. Allison even mentioned that this was a very unconventional way of entering The Vow, because normally the process was far more involved and had certain protocols. However, Allison's haste would ultimately be her demise, since she lacked foresight and got sloppy, not to mention she was arrogant.

Little by little, I was beginning to trust the NXIVM community, but I always kept a little notepad in my mind to keep track of anything strange that I would notice. There was a manipulative way of doing things—it involved long-term indoctrination (the "long game"). We began to act as recruiters and could find people who were interested in personal development, particularly women who were badasses, who wanted to grow and would benefit from NXIVM. Behind the scenes, however, there were more plans and strategies—some of which varied from person to person to secure more recruits.

With respect to The Vow, the recruitment process started off by just making a list of women, then there were "warm calls" to plant the seeds. Some of the time we were working with women who had familiarity with NXIVM, or others who had no relationship to NXIVM whatsoever. Next, the warm call became a "hot call" where we told them about the "collateral." Part of this process also hinged on the fact that it was "all or nothing"—you either joined this secret society within NXIVM, or you were left out. Perhaps a bit of the allure of joining The

Vow was the fact that you had no idea what you would be missing if you stayed out. The promise, in other words, of *something* exclusive, was a lure.

Once the collateral was secured, the woman was then isolated. The secret of The Vow could not be talked about besides with one's master. This is part of long game of training, indoctrination, reading books like *Chasm of Fire* and journaling about it. I thought that I was evolving and becoming independent. The Vow made me feel different from other people. There were more intensives, more ESP courses, and more grooming.

The women valued by The Vow were very influential and attractive. Allison asked us to "think of an app we could do to attract other women." This was an idea for an app, or a game, or some other type of lure, to have women join their group and continue to be influenced. They targeted women to have voting power, buying power, and the ability to control and influence these women. People on my list were women I admired and respected, including spiritual healers, models, and entrepreneurs.

Robin was the only one I ever recruited which in reality, was Allison's recruit because Allison had been so eager to get Robin into The

Vow and did the enlisting. I never participated in recruiting any other women, besides putting names on a list, and it never went any farther than that. With Robin now in The Vow, I had to deal with the fact that I, too, had a slave that I was responsible for. The assignment I had to give Robin was one that I already had completed, which was to read the book *Chasm of Fire* and have her do a book report. After Vancouver, I flew to Albany for a week to decompress after completing The Source. I stayed at 7 General's Way. I was even more open, raw, and had a lot of deep emotional trauma to process. I found myself oftentimes at Allison's apartment, which she dubbed "The Womb," crying profusely on her couch, as I processed my trauma. I felt closer than ever to Allison and India. They suggested that I actually move to Albany to work on myself, and that I could live in Allison's house at 7 General's Way for free. But I was not convinced; I had just signed with a new agent, was booking jobs like crazy, and was about take my career to the next level, although something deep inside me was not quite happy in LA.

For now, being in Albany was an opportunity to go on another walk with Keith. In between now and the last time I had seen him, I had sent him the business plan for the t-shirt company. Again, we went on a walk to further detail the endeavor. Keith said that my business plan looked good, but the element I included about charity was something to be mindful about because charities were often tax shelters for the wealthy—so I should choose the charity wisely. He gave me some notes and wanted me to resend the business plan, but overall, it looked like things were moving in the right direction.

The day that I flew back to LA, I received a message from Keith saying, "If you're serious about this t-shirt company, the sooner you come back to Albany, the better." After receiving this semi-cryptic message, I knew what he really meant—and that was that I needed to move to Albany if I wanted to start this t-shirt company. I felt ecstatic. After I received that message, I tapped inwards and asked myself what I should do. The answer I got was that I needed to move to Albany. It was a hard yes, but inside, I said: "Fuck it—I'm moving to Albany."

To me, this was the beginning of a new chapter and an epic adventure. I had never really lived outside of California—there was something about the peace and quiet, the big open sky of Albany. To others, it might have seemed boring and weird, but to me, it felt like a reprieve. This would be my sabbatical. An opportunity for me to work on myself, to now be mentored by this self-proclaimed genius and develop a company as an entrepreneur, that I anticipated I could also make a decent income from. In my mind, after a year of doing that, I could go to New York City (which I fell in love with), or go back to LA, or wherever life would take me.

Upon returning to LA, I had to tell my boyfriend, Tej, that I had planned to move to Albany. This would have been a harder conversation if our relationship wasn't already on the rocks. Even though my career was flourishing, my personal life was suffering deeply. I wasn't happy. It was time for me to go pursue something that was for my overall happiness and well-being without having to consider anyone else.

A Northeast Winter

On January 11, 2017, I moved to Albany. I packed up my things and brought my cat Niko (short for Nikola) to begin our new life. Niko was sadly diagnosed with Feline Leukemia. Niko and I were soul bonded to one another, and even though he was sick, we still managed to run around the house and play tag. Niko was a unique cat—he would sit on command, a wizard of sorts in cat-form. Even though I knew he had leukemia, Niko was not aware of his medical condition. Even still, I sought to give him the best life that I could. Even people who didn't like cats were attracted to Niko. Niko was never aggressive with anyone and yet, when Keith came over to the house, Niko growled at him. Keith claimed he had "power over cats" and could "make them go to sleep on command," although never did I see him attempt to do so.

When I landed in the Albany airport, I felt familiar with the place I would be moving to. That familiarity, however, did not make it any less strange to be away from home. LA was the type of place that people moved *to*, not moved away *from*. Now I was living in a small, cold, northeastern town where the most important place was Walmart, and the average temperature was less than 14 degrees.

India picked me up from the airport and drove me out to Clifton Park. By that evening, I again ended up in Allison's house at 7 General's Way. This house was a typical suburban home with two stories, like you would see on a sitcom. It was cozy and had a communal atmosphere. Now that I would be living in the community full-time, I expected that I would be treated well, and anticipated not having to do too much on my own. However, I noticed that there were multiple people living in Allison's house—all of whom were in NXIVM but were somewhat transient. It felt like a sorority house, full of people who would come and go.

There was food labeled in the fridge with people's names on it. In fact, the fridge was broken and did not shut properly. There was a piece of brown, coarse string attached to the door handle, which was wrapped around the fridge, in order to keep the door shut. I began to survey the house, trying to decide where I should put my things, including my cat and belongings. There was a renovated basement underneath the house where I put my stuff down. "Well, I'm here," I thought to myself.

I needed to decompress after suddenly arriving in this place where I would be living in an unknown environment. The only thing that connected us was NXIVM; otherwise, we were complete strangers. I felt like an alien. After dropping my stuff off, India took me to the Walmart to grab some food. It all felt very underwhelming. But receiving love from India—who was so happy and excited to have me there—felt warm, so I played along.

There was no immediate plan except to get me there and allow things to unfold. People were already so involved with NXIVM on the ground, including working in committees and doing independent work. There seemed to be committees for everything: poetry committee, food committee, art committee, safety committee, a committee on committees, and so on. The committee leaders were like Stepford housewives, eager to gain new members and add them to an overbearing group chat thread. Although everyone was busy, it did not necessarily feel organized. There were people buzzing about as if they all had direction, but most meetings were small and informal, composed of loosely organized subgroups that wanted you to become a part of their mission.

In The Vow, the first assignment was the "good morning and good night" text messages. The second assignment was a 3-minute cold shower before I did anything. The next assignment was to weigh myself and send it to my master before I ate in the morning. The next one was called "*1 to 27*," an assignment that included all of the above, as well as a twenty-minute walk of contemplation and intermittent fasting, which we were required to complete every day. Some of the other assignments were journaling assignments, like asking: "What is a wise woman?" or "How do I see my life in 5 to 10 years?" and other questions like that. Other assignments included "acts of care," which were framed as ways of empathizing or thinking about your master and how to make their life easier. You could buy them a gift or do something nice for them. I knew India liked poetry and memes, so I would sporadically send her those. I also gifted her earrings and nails (mani-pedi), or just helped her however I could.

Then, there was the "calorie-deficiency" diet. At the time, this diet didn't seem strange to me because I was required to listen to a podcast about Ramadan, which discussed fasting as a way of sacrificing for your higher power. This is how they indoctrinated us into believing we were doing something that was better for us, in order to conceal their actual intentions. In addition, being in the entertainment and modeling industry, calorie-counting was not abnormal; in fact, it was very expected in that context. Lastly, it also played into the struggles I had with eating disorders in the past, like anorexia and exercise bulimia, or just chewing food and spitting it out. The idea of calorie-counting was something familiar to me, though in hindsight it was neither appropriate, nor healthy.

At first, I was told to measure my calories. During my initial phase, I was told to keep my diet to **1,000** calories per day. On my phone, I downloaded an app that recorded my caloric intake. Recording the calories was necessary in order to know how many calories I consumed. Over time, the amount I could consume gradually decreased from **1,000** to **800** calories, and then to as little as **500** calories per day. I often "failed" this task, which became an issue for me. It just made no sense.

Although this was framed as a "discipline assignment," there was a level of seriousness to it that made me feel suspicious. In order to determine an accurate number of calories, I saw people taking out scales and weighing their winter and acorn squash. These were *already* low-calorie foods. Taring out cups and bowls, people were whipping out their scales to determine how much food they could eat, measuring it, and taking pictures. I eventually was required to take a picture of what I was eating and then use an equation to determine the calories. When I had taken the photo and calculated the calories, I would send a text: "Master, may I eat this many calories?" with the picture and the equation.

Obviously, there was a dark side to this diet. I started to hear how women were not menstruating, as well as losing their hair. I reached the conclusion that these women were suffering because they weren't eating enough. "What they're doing isn't healthy," I told myself. I wanted to rebel against this and was very frustrated. One time, I prepared food to eat, which I took a picture of and sent to India. "Master, may I eat this?" I asked. I was so hungry and tempted to eat the food but patiently waited to receive a text message back. It felt like hours went by. There was no response. I waited longer. The frustration grew.

At some point, I let myself calm down and eventually the hunger pains subsided. Later, I told India about what had happened, describing the feeling of how I let my anger control me. I thought I was going to die due to the hunger I felt. There was a lesson here, however, that was helpful. They weren't just starving me to put me through a painful experience. I was having an entire temper tantrum, "How dare she not answer me?" By having to be disciplined and obedient, I overcame some of my anger and entitlement, as I witnessed myself having the tantrum. Although there were some ulterior motives, I admittedly learned from this experience and became more empowered within myself (though I do not think this necessarily was their intention). I wasn't letting my hunger control me.

At one point, I was taking fish oil supplements and many other natural vitamins. I asked India if I needed to count them in my diet because one soft gel was almost **100** calories. India told me that I did have to count the fish oil supplements in my diet, which infuriated me more. I disregarded what she said for the most part and listened to my body. I knew that they didn't know better than me when it came to my health.

Looking at it now, I believe NXIVM was trying to break us down to make us more susceptible to being influenced. Not only did it break us down psychologically, but all these tasks had the desired effect: The Vow wanted us to look a certain way. The Vow liked women who were skinny and were willing to tailor their bodies to its needs, including our grooming regimen. India told us that removing our pubic hair was an act of "violence" on women's bodies, encouraged by the porn industry. The Vow wanted to take control of everything to shape us into exactly what it wanted, like The Wizard of Oz.

Everything happened so fast. There was never a moment of thinking about making the "right" or the "wrong" choice. I never necessarily viewed it in a black and white way. From an intellectual standpoint, I lived my life and made my way through the NXIVM world. It never dawned on me that things would be viewed in such a stark light after NXIVM was over. In other words, it was not just one thing that happened that stood out to me as "bad," but over the course of time, many events led me to believe something was not right.

At volleyball, both men and women would go up to Keith and kiss him on the lips. Naturally, that seemed suspect. It was just odd to see adults kissing this hobbit of a man on the lips, while wearing a full-on volleyball outfit, headband and all. But everyone was doing it. And these weren't strange folks but rather, people who were wealthy, ambitious, and attractive, who had moved their entire lives to Albany—and they adored Keith from the stands and kissed him on the lips, too. Some of the women were successful and beautiful, some of them were mothers and others were single. Regardless, I kept thinking: "This is *their* life? This is what they do?" I could not imagine being in their shoes, because theirs was not the life I aspired to have.

Suddenly, it began to strike me as odd because nothing about NXIVM would outwardly promote this kind of unconventional behavior. There was nothing about it that was overt—rather it seemed to be under the surface. The NXIVM I knew was more strait-laced and had a professional atmosphere. There was nothing about it that was like a hippie commune, where polyamory, free love, and communal living would be expected. I tried to reserve my own judgment: maybe they were just more open with their intimacy than I would have expected. The indoctrination of misogyny in the curriculum was very subtle, especially in the beginning. I wasn't cynical, nor did I suspect that there was anything nefarious going on, so I was not primed to think there was a problem. Except watching adult strangers—straight men and women—kissing one man, Keith, on the lips, for no apparent reason, struck me as odd.

One night at the Sports Barn, while Keith was playing volleyball, I remember hearing him make a few off-color sex jokes. It's difficult to remember even what the jokes were about, but the comments were made in a context that felt entirely inappropriate. The tone and conversation were just on the edge of comfort, and because of that, it felt like these comments were designed to desensitize us. Initially, Keith never made any overt remarks about sex or approached me directly. From what I later learned, he preferred to be chased by women—a sort of ego-stroking strategy.

Since I have dealt with predators in the past, I am familiar with their behavior and psychological tactics. I have a sixth sense for them. One night, I was at volleyball with a big group, watching the game at the Sports Barn. It was cold outside; I was wearing my big green parka inside the gym. At one point, as the group was talking, Keith stood next to me. In the middle of the conversation that people were having, out of nowhere, he stretched out his index finger and—without even looking at me—traced a circle around my abdomen area, over the parka. It was a small and unassuming gesture. However, he was in my personal space, not as an attack, but as a way of asserting authority over my body. It was as if there was a spotlight on me, but no one could see it. It felt very intimate in a way that I did not invite in or bring upon myself. I kept this memory in the back of my head.

At one point, Allison asked me what I thought about Keith. We were driving into town together. Out of nowhere, she quizzed me: "How do you feel about Keith? What are your thoughts on him?" I had little personal experience with Keith at that point, beyond our walks. "He seems cool, like a nice, caring person, who is interesting." But I could tell that Allison was trying to pull something more out of me. I just didn't have very much to give her. This guy looked like Golem—only Golem was skinnier.

Nevertheless, Allison's questioning planted the seeds for what would happen down the road. One day she said, "Keith wants to see how you are doing," which was a sort of signpost that made my thoughts swirl. Keith worked through other people, so the energy he projected did not raise any eyebrows. Not to mention, everyone was brainwashed and indoctrinated to worship him. Another "act of care for my 'M,'" India, was to help her with the company she started with Keith called "Delegates." Not only did I become a delegate, and worked for her, but I also helped format her business plan and some of her guidelines. I was helping her for free because she was my master, but I did get paid when I was working as a delegate. My tasks included making deliveries to the NXIVM community, as a "task rabbit," getting paid to run errands or pick up people from the airport. I started to make deliveries to Keith's house. Over time, I was making tons of deliveries specifically to Keith's house, which I began to notice and felt suspicious of; it seemed beyond a coincidence.

After my second delivery to Keith's house, Keith invited me to come in for a conversation. "It's not my house," he said, acting nonchalant and cool about the entire conversation, but gesturing as if we could have a brief talk inside. I was delivering pizza to the house, which someone had ordered for him (because Keith never lifted a finger or was accountable for anything on his own). "Huh," I thought, "this is somewhat uncomfortable." It began to feel like my trips to Keith's house were not a coincidence at all.

Allison had me write out all the high-value things I'd received in my life and how I had accomplished my goals. "Did you use your sexuality to achieve those things?" she asked. Initially, it felt like something to be ashamed of; it was not as if she was insinuating, I was using my body for work. "How did flirting or my looks afford me certain things?" I had an expensive designer purse that an ex-boyfriend bought for me. Allison wanted to know: "Why did your ex-boyfriend buy this for you?" Allison wanted a profile of my sexuality, because she knew it was a source of pain due to the fact that I had long suffered from abandonment, which created self-destructive behaviors. Her strategy, in other words, was to prey upon my insecurities—the abuse I suffered, the withholding of love from my family —and in doing so, she was suggesting that I use my sexuality for good causes. This was a grooming tactic and segue into the "special assignment."

One day, Allison called me from San Diego, where she was rehearsing for a play. I had my headphones on while going on a walk, but raced back to 7 General's Way where I stormed excitedly down into the basement where I was staying. Allison started the conversation by saying, "Everyone in the community loves you. You fit right in." My heart was racing, and my Spidey-senses were going off. My intuition was telling me something big was about to happen. Allison continued, "India and I talked it over and decided we want to give you a 'special assignment.' This is unique; very rarely does anyone get an assignment like this. It's an honor and a privilege, but it's a top-secret assignment, so no one can know about it."

As I listened, I became more and more confused as my heart was pounding out of my chest. "The assignment is to seduce Keith and have him take a naked picture of you to prove that you did it." The room started spinning and the walls felt like they were melting. Suddenly, the world I had built was completely destroyed. Feeling a sense of shock and betrayal, and confusion, I asked Allison, "Does Keith know about The Vow?" Up until that point, I had only ever thought of Keith as my mentor—this seemed so bizarre and wrong. I thought he was like a celibate monk. "No," she replied, "Keith doesn't know about The Vow."

Chaos and confusion ensued. "What is the point of this assignment?" I asked. "Don't you still have issues with men?" Allison asked. "Yeah, I mean, I guess—although I've been working on it." "Well," Allison ruminated, "this assignment will get rid of your *disintegrations*—all your issues around being sexually abused." "Oh, shit," I quickly realized and said to myself. "I accidentally joined a cult, and the leader wants to have sex with me." In this moment I experienced what is known as an "ego death." The old facade of my LA persona, clout and existence had just been executed, military style. This was literally my worst nightmare with joining NXIVM come to life. The most cliché and embarrassing thing that my ego could not hide or run from.

In that instant, I felt the rage of my inner momma bear protecting the Little Jess inside of me. The fact that she would try to use my pain and trauma to further create more harm and abuse to me and my inner child infuriated me. In my mind, I said, "You fucking bitch." In that moment, I realized Allison was dead-serious about doing this assignment; she anticipated that I would do it—I flipped a switch and turned on "Ninja Jess" and began to play as a double-agent. There was no way in hell I was going to do that assignment. What I thought I was getting out of the badass woman's bootcamp training was going into full effect.

Allison tried to comfort me by offering time to talk and counsel if I wanted to talk about the assignment with her and India. I played dumb and acted bewildered to give the impression that I would go along with it eventually. I knew that she would not be forceful, in that moment. The last thing I heard Allison say before ending the phone call was, "And I give you permission to enjoy it." I could feel the sinister intention vibrating from the tone of her voice. She knew exactly what she was doing.

Primal Ordeal

Ninja Jess was activated as soon as I had received my special assignment from Allison. Ninja Jess is not an alter-ego per se, but she lives inside of me; she has the blood of my warrior ancestors coursing through her veins. Ninja Jess started her training process very young, by going through the hard experiences she had, including those that motivated her to continue to survive. She's hyper-aware and has incredible perception. When I got off the phone with Allison, Ninja Jess was ready to take swift action.

While Ninja Jess was ready, my ego was laid out, K.O.'d on the mat, down for the count. My initial reaction to the assignment was utter confusion: "Why would I want to do *that* with my mentor?" None of this made sense. Allison's praise of me was like a dozen empty compliments, stacked on top of each other. It was as if each compliment was chosen carefully to make me feel as if I was a shining light, desperately trying to win me over and convince me of things. It was clear she was up to something. Whatever "light" I had felt turned to utter and complete darkness when she issued the assignment. It was twisted, nauseating, and sinister, so much so that I just could not wrap my head around it. If it hadn't been obvious before this conversation, Allison's intent was depraved: to groom me for their ultimate gain. There is no other explanation for what she did, but she was a monster helping another monster. To place me in a position like that, through this assignment, was pure evil.

I happened to see India on a walk in Clifton Park, shortly after receiving the assignment from Allison. I told India about what Allison had said and asked her if she would tell me about her experience. At first, India looked like a deer in headlights and said she didn't want to talk about her experience at all. I now realize it was cowardice compounded by her guilt and shame. However, the one tidbit she was willing to share was that she was surprised at how "amazing" Keith's body was. She mentioned that Keith prefers to be "chased" by women. She didn't offer much information either way and only added to the confusion. I didn't know if she was just that severely brainwashed or enjoyed this underbelly of a lifestyle. Beyond being my "Master", I considered India a close friend. I trusted her. She was the whole reason why I joined The Vow. I thought she would protect me—never did I ever think she would be a part of a plan to compromise me and cause me harm. At this point I realized she was not a true friend and was not to be trusted. She knew what she was doing recruiting me into The Vow.

At the time, I did not have all the information about what was going on inside The Vow. All I knew was that them giving me this assignment was very telling that something was seriously wrong. The Vow knew that I wanted to become an elevated person—that personal development was my highest value—and they also knew about my vulnerabilities, which would allow them to wield considerable influence over me. I recognize that these insecurities were a fact of my life, but they do not define me. I am a survivor, not a victim. Yet, because of my experiences, The Vow sought to groom me, to eventually subject me to Keith's most sinister sexual desires. And I refused to be a part of it— Nothing in my body, mind and Spirit was going to allow that to happen.

At times, I wondered if the process they used to indoctrinate me into The Vow was the same for everyone else. When I thought about the collateral, I had given them, it was information about myself that made me vulnerable—as open and transparent as I am—which led them to prey upon me in a *certain way*. There was a unique process to get me, just as there was a similarly unique process of getting everyone else. No two people were the same.

*

As soon as I hung up with Allison, I opened up my laptop in my little basement room. The walls were still spinning. I gained a sense of composure as my computer booted up. I was now in mission mode. I went online to research what I could find about NXIVM. This special assignment was a tip-off. Tucked away, on the eleventh page of Google, was an article about NXIVM and an alleged harem. After reading the article, the assignment now seemed to make sense. The cogs in my head began to turn. How could I get out of this situation unscathed?

They messed with the wrong person. By this point, so much of my life was tied up in NXIVM, but I now knew I had to escape at whatever cost. The problem was that any noticeable change in my behavior would sound the alarm. I could have taken my chances by just walking away, but I don't run away from situations like this—when it comes to fight or flight, I fight. I also knew that NXIVM had considerable power and money, so I knew I had to be smart for my own protection and safety, as well as for the others in NXIVM whom I wanted to help get out. NXIVM's financial resources had destroyed dissidents in the past by employing a powerful legal team and private investigators, who would bankrupt you with lawsuits, harassment, and an overwhelming sense of dread. There was no mercy shown for the people who "wronged" NXIVM.

Luckily, I had an out. A few weeks back, I had booked my plane ticket for a family trip to Mexico and was about to book an extra ticket for my cat because someone in the house was allergic. I had already cleared the trip with India and Allison, and my plan was to leave in the coming weeks anyway. Yet, if I wasn't going to come back, I knew that I couldn't take all my stuff away at the same time, or else they would suspect me. Regardless of my possessions that I'd have to leave behind, my cat Niko would be coming with me no matter what.

To move ahead without raising any eyebrows, I played along, but at the same time, realized I could still help others along the way. It was crucial for me to pretend I was still in The Vow because the longer I played along, the more time I had to gather evidence. I started by accessing the Dropbox folder where Allison stored the collateral belonging to her group. That folder contained photos, videos, and documents. New collateral was due on the first of every month and it stayed online for 24 hours. I wanted the collateral as protection against anyone who would try to threaten me, but more importantly, as evidence to show what they were doing was wrong.

I still needed to be careful. I was wary that if I downloaded anything off the Dropbox folder, they would be able to detect that I was saving the collateral and would question me about what I was doing. It would be obvious I was collecting the files for some other purpose. Instead of risking it, I went stealth and took undetectable screenshots of the collateral on my phone.

Because I had a mentee (Robin), I was given access to the collateral Dropbox folder and entrusted to keep it safe. Robin did not have access to the files online, so she sent me her collateral, and I would post it, along with my own, to the folder. My instincts to do all this came from an understanding that life is unpredictable. Your worst nightmares can come true. I had the perfect little world when I was a child, then my mother left. When my mother left, the world I had known suddenly disappeared, and I realized that I needed to protect myself. The environment I had growing up, especially living through what I had already endured, the things that transpired, made my impulses strong.

I kickstarted the process of separating myself from NXIVM. I flew back home and landed in California, en route to Mexico for my family vacation. I drove down to Mexico from LA with Tej. On the drive down, things were pleasant—life almost felt normal again. There was a caravan with us on the trip, all of us driving in separate cars, including my dad, stepmom, and my cousins. My dad bought us a bunch of walkie-talkies, which we used to keep track of each other, but mostly to crack jokes with. I knew that I could not tell any of them about what was happening—no one except Tej knew, and even then, I made him swear he would tell no one.

Usually, when Tej asked me about ESP, I was reluctant to talk about it. I'd say, "You don't really know anything about NXIVM because you haven't taken a course." My icy reception to his intrigue was my elitist way of defending the parts of NXIVM I was sure he would not understand. But this time when Tej asked me about ESP, I was open to talking about it. Tej had printed a bunch of paperwork and had compiled a dossier of research about Keith and NXIVM. He started off talking about Keith and the negative things he had heard. Instead of brushing him off, I looked at Tej and said, "Yes. Something has happened." He looked shocked, but also relieved that I was now present and awakened again. I was still participating in readiness drills but had started to go "dark" and distance myself from the group.

I told him about the special assignment I received recently. Tej was protective of me and wanted to make sure that I was being smart, so we agreed not to talk to anyone else about this until I was out safely. However, I attached the collateral in an email to Tej with a subject line: "DO NOT OPEN THIS," and in the body of the message, I wrote, "Bitch, don't kill my vibe." I stored other files in a folder on my computer and labeled it: "TAKE THEM DOWN." I used Facebook to find people I thought might threaten me and find their families, too. This was done in case anything happened to me—I would blow everything up by sending the collateral to their families, so they would know what their child was up to in their little "humanitarian group" down in Albany.

The trip to Mexico lasted less than a week, so to continue playing along, I told India that my grandmother had cancer, which required me to stay in California for a while to support her. They knew I was close with my family and that, as a humanitarian company, it would go against their ethic to deny me time with my family. One of my grandmothers was sick, so my story had the benefit of being true (though my grandmother was not actually that ill). In addition, I was bankrupted by NXIVM and had no money whatsoever—all of it was being spent for the courses I was enrolled in. After we left Mexico, I headed back up to LA and bounced around different friends' places.

Meanwhile, Allison was in San Diego at the same time. She was performing in a play at the Old Globe Theater in downtown. Ironically, the play Allison was in, entitled *Red Velvet*, was described as "transporting audiences to a turbulent backstage world of London's Theatre Royal in the early 1800s," in which the greatest actor of his generation "can't go on tonight as Othello, and his company is in *disarray* . . .". The irony was that, as Allison was acting in this play, our own turbulent backstage was unfolding and the entire company was in *disarray*. Everything about NXIVM began to fall apart within a month.

Allison had been in San Diego for some time, and she borrowed my car, while I used hers in Albany. I took a train down to San Diego where my aunt lives as I was ordered to watch Allison's play. When my aunt picked me up from the train station, I didn't tell her anything about my situation with NXIVM. Later that night, I went to the Old Globe to watch Allison's play. No one in NXIVM had been checking in on me when they thought my grandmother was sick, especially India and Allison. In fact, all the expected "check-ins" that were usually required to text day-in and day-out had fallen away, as I was pulling myself out.

Even though we were always expected to be in contact with our master, I was still participating in readiness drills, but slowly began to "go dark" more often. "Going dark" was a term we used when anyone was on an airplane or out of reach. "I'm going to the hospital now. Going dark," I would text India. Going dark gave me the flexibility to stop the ridiculous calorie counting and the good night and good morning text messages day after day. I did the minimum requirement, but slowly began to get my power back. I also needed to get the practical parts of my life back, including my car. Even though my grandmother was ill, India still tried to sway me away from moving back to California. "Are you sure this is the most caring thing you can do?" she asked. If I was a better version of myself, would I be helping my family more? I brushed her off firmly: "My family is really important to me. I need to be there." The groundwork had already been laid.

That night, at the Old Globe, my ticket to Allison's play were at will-call. I arrived close to the start of the play, in order to avoid being around the other slaves. I was seated away from everyone else, away from the rest of the group. I felt anxious and annoyed that I had to be there. It was as if I was an actor in a play, acting as the disobedient one, even though deep down I had already gone far beyond disobedience—I was

126

no longer in their orbit whatsoever. I sat through the play, waiting for it to be over.

After the final act, Allison instructed India to take me on a walk. While on the walk, I asked India about my collateral, and what would happen if I wanted to leave NXIVM. "India," I said, "in the beginning, you told me that the collateral was only there to protect the secrecy of the group, so if I wanted to leave, nothing would happen to my collateral, right?" India dismissed my concerns. "Well, you're already in the group," she said, giving a non-answer. "I know," I responded calmly, while at the same time, dismissing her, "but you told me the collateral was there only to protect the secrecy of the group." I repeated the question again. "So, if I wanted to leave and didn't say anything about The Vow, nothing would happen to my collateral, right?" India was visibly distressed and suddenly it became heated. "You're *already* in the group," she insisted, then continued: "It's too late. You made a lifetime commitment." I looked her directly in face, stone cold, piercing into her eyes. "Are you threatening me? Because I feel like I'm being threatened right now."

By that point, India and I had walked to the front of Allison's apartment. Allison came down to meet us, but she immediately detected something was wrong. India was still visibly taken aback by my questions about the collateral, seemingly at a loss for words. I needed my car. Allison told me my car was parked in a lot nearby, so I left them and went looking for it. I spent hours roaming the streets in an Uber, scanning the area and moving on to neighboring lots where it could have been parked. After a fruitless search, I called Allison to ask for help. Allison said she couldn't remember where the car was and told me to come back the next day. This was obviously very convenient for me.

The next day, I came back to Allison's apartment to get my car. Allison, myself, and two of the other slaves, dropped India off at the train station. I didn't get out of the car to help India with her bags, which enraged Allison to the point where she began to chastise me, calling me "entitled" and "selfish" for my unwillingness to help my master with her bags. After we dropped India off, Allison and I, with the two other slaves, drove to the parking garage where my car was parked. My car was in a completely different place than Allison had told me the night before—there was no way I would've found it without her. Now, at the correct parking garage, both Allison and I got out to walk around to look for the car.

As we were walking, Allison acknowledged that they had been pushing hard on me, but also that she had noticed I was distant of late.

"What's happened to you?" she asked. "I thought you were invested and committed to this." She also pointed out that they were still figuring out how to "do this" at the same time. "We're learning what's helpful for you guys and what's not." I could feel something prickly happening. I told Allison that my grandmother was sick, which is why I had been distant, but also that the latest assignment had freaked me out. I told her that I read a bunch of stuff about NXIVM online, and that I believed it.

Once she had heard me, Allison played the role of the victim as if she were in a cancelled soap opera. She implied that I was oppressing her, especially once I told her I looked up all the information about NXIVM and Keith online. "So, you believe that I am an accomplice to a child molester?" she asked. "Yes," I said pointedly, "that's exactly what I think." Allison and I found my car, and we both got in. Allison was suddenly full of malice, as she offered to pay for the parking so that way it wouldn't seem like she was using me. "I just want to leave, Allison." I said. We spent the entirety of the ride in silence. After we exited the garage, she got out and walked to the car where the other slaves were parked.

*

After I left Allison, I drove back to LA. Allison knew I had a close relationship with Jenna, who was unaware of what was happening, and told me Jenna was also in San Diego to watch the play. I could see that Allison was using Jenna as a lure, telling me, "Jenna would love to see you." I already knew Jenna wanted to see me. Allison asked me if I could give her and Jenna a ride back to her parents' place in Orange County. I wanted to save Jenna, so I drove back to San Diego, to check on her and seize the opportunity to plant seeds in her mind that something was up.

Jenna was my main confidante in Albany and one of the reasons why I even wanted to move there. Even though Jenna and I weren't *officially* introduced in The Vow (it was obvious we were both in it), we would often confide in each other, sometimes using codes or nicknames. When we were having a bad time in The Vow, we called it "Le Suck." Jenna and I had a special relationship; sometimes we would be naughty together. We'd eat things we weren't supposed to (like finger sandwiches) and delightfully ignore our requirement to count calories.

Even though I had raised concerns with Allison, I was still playing along, meaning I was giving collateral and trying to stay organized. I gave the most basic collateral I could think of. I drove

Allison and Jenna up to Orange County. On that drive, Allison told me that I was the first person who had challenged her and that she had to change her tactics in order to get me to comply with what she wanted. Allison was buttering me up. Her goal was to preserve my relationship with The Vow by any means possible.

One of the last times I saw Allison was at a dinner near Brentwood. It was Allison, Gabriella, and Robin—I came later. Gabriella and Jenna were fawning over Allison. After dinner, Allison, Robin, and myself went to get frozen yogurt. I was annoyed, but I was there to check on Gabriella and Robin—to assess the situation. Eventually, Robin left, and it was just Allison and me. We walked to another parking garage. Allison started to talk. "Because we're still figuring out how to do this program, you can do this however you want to, Jess . . ." she said. That was never an option before—there was no customized, make-your-own-fucking-Vow-program. Allison continued: "If you want to do it fast or slow—you can do it *however* you want to." She had completely changed her tune. She said she wanted to help me.

After letting Allison talk for a while, I put the final stake in her heart once and for all: "No, thank you. I want to live my life as an artist, as a human, make my own mistakes and learn from them. There's nothing you can do to help me," I said in a matter-of-fact tone. "I'm going to Hawaii." We sat in her rental car for a second to finish the conversation. Allison's crocodile tears streamed down her face, as she took on a tragic soap opera tone again. "I just *feel* like I failed you." She made me cringe. "Well," I said, "it's your choice. It's nothing personal, but if you want to feel that way, it's completely up to you." That was a dagger: there are no inherent victims in ESP.

It felt so good to use the lessons of ESP against her.

Where There's Smoke, There's Fire

That was the last time I saw Allison. Around that time, India was planning to be in California for her birthday and invited me to her party in Malibu. Before India came out, she told me there was a special ceremony on June 1st in Albany. I told her I'd come, but in actuality, there was no way in hell I would go. I was so done with all of them and their rituals, ceremonies, and their mindless rules.

While I waited for India's birthday party, I spent some time with my mother. Together, my mom and I went to a coffee shop where I sat down and wrote a letter, almost like a resignation letter, that I addressed to India. If there was any question about my intention to leave The Vow, this letter would be the official notice that I was done. Once I was finished with the letter, I spun the laptop over so my mom could read it over. She read it and asked, "Is everything OK, honey?" I told her I was fine. She still looked slightly concerned. "It's just that this letter is a little aggressive. Is something wrong? You know, I'm your mom, so if somethings wrong, you need to tell me."

We exchanged a knowing glance, but still, I told her everything was fine. "No," she said, "you *need* to tell me if something is wrong."

This went on for a few moments. "Do I need to make a phone call?" she asked. Again, I told her I was fine, I had it all under control. "Are you sure?" she asked one more time. "Yes, I got it. Thank you, but if I need you to make a phone call, I'll let you know." I finished the letter and decided I'd just give it to India in person. But a week later, I missed her birthday party. And then Runyon Canyon happened.

*

May 31, 2017, is a day I will never forget. A day or two leading up to the 31st, I had a vision. Out of nowhere, I began to visualize India's mom, Catherine Oxenberg, whom I had never met before. I had seen photos of her that India showed me, but I never gave much thought about meeting her. This vision was strong, like a premonition, and it stuck out in my mind. I pictured Catherine alone in a faded room. Somehow, I just knew that I was going to meet her.

On the 31st, I was planning to hike in Runyon Canyon with Robin. Runyon is a popular hiking destination in Hollywood. It's a scenic route where a lot of people—tourists, celebrities, couples, and dog walkers—can be found meeting up for a casual outdoor workout. Leading up to our hike, I knew I could make a last ditch effort to plant seeds in Robin's head, as she was about to become India's slave. I wanted to stop Robin from being forced to do something she did not want to do. I wanted to remind her she didn't have to do *anything* she didn't want to. I wanted to see her in person before I moved to Hawaii and before she was left to be on her own in The Vow.

It was the early afternoon when I parked my car and met up with Robin at the base of Runyon. Robin and I began hiking up the hill, catching up with one another about our lives. We had just started the "medium" difficulty route when suddenly Robin turned pale white, as if she'd seen a ghost. Her phone was ringing, but she was screening the calls, which were coming from Catherine Oxenberg. Finally, Robin received a text message. I could read the anxiety on her face, as if she had just seen death. "Are you O.K.?" I asked, "What's going on?" Robin handed me the phone and I read the text: "Please don't go to Albany tomorrow," Catherine said. "You may be involved with illegal activities happening there. The women you're involved with are very dangerous." As soon as I read that text message, I felt liberated; I took it as a sign from God and I knew that it was safe for me to say everything because Catherine had just cast the first stone and there was no turning back. I told Robin everything.

We progressed further and further up the trail, nearing the top of Runyon. I told Robin about the special assignment I received and how everything didn't feel right. I told her how I was also handling things my own way—without giving her any specifics about the collateral I collected. Then suddenly, Bonnie called Robin. Bonnie was an actress and Mark Vicente's wife who had recently distanced herself from NXIVM, after being a high-level Proctor for many years. Bonnie also instructed Robin not to go to Albany, re-emphasizing how dangerous it would be and that she cared about her. "Can we trust you?" Bonnie asked Robin over the phone. Everyone was afraid of NXIVM and the repercussions for defecting.

Robin began to cry. The situation was so overwhelming. "Well," she said finally, "Jessica is here with me. She already left The Vow and we can trust her." At that point, we all decided it would be best to talk in-person. Bonnie, myself, Robin and Catherine, along with a few other women, met up in Santa Monica for a secret meeting. India was nowhere in sight; in fact, Catherine had tried to make an intervention at her birthday party a few days prior. At the party, Catherine went around and collected people's phone numbers after telling India that she wouldn't be an accomplice to recruiting new women at the party for NXIVM's abuse.

That's how Catherine ended up getting Robin's phone number. However, India denied anything was wrong, telling Catherine she was trying to do something good. But Catherine persisted.

At the meeting in Santa Monica, we all began to share our experiences, seated around a back patio in a small restaurant. Everyone had already heard a lot of things: some women had received "hot" calls about this "special" women's group, Catherine was concerned about her daughter, and Bonnie had been in NXIVM for years, long suspecting something was awry. But none of them were in The Vow except Robin and me. When it was my turn, I told everyone about The Vow and the special assignment I had. High-intensity, and terrifying, I started to hear about how they put women in cages, and some of the other sadistic punishments handed out.

I heard details about the branding, as well as other information received from people who were not in the group. I told them that I would be moving to Hawaii and that I would help as much as I could. Shit had just hit the fan. I knew that NXIVM was crumbling, and that Keith's freedom was on borrowed time.

That was the first meeting. Then we went to work. We wanted to get people's stories written down so we could go to the FBI and share everything we knew. There was a group of ex-ESPians who, once they heard about all this, came out of the woodwork and started calling one another to talk. We hoped that the FBI would begin their investigation after they heard from us. At that point, I had no idea what purpose I would serve. I had friends who were involved intimately with Keith, and because I was a trusted person, I encouraged them to talk to our lawyer. I thought this would be the main way I could help at this stage.

We knew that it would take a lot to convince people that NXIVM was *not* what they thought it was. Even after women showed their brands, some people dismissed it as a "choice," and suggested it was all about "building strength and character." We were far from being out of the woods. Far from it. Some people were so indoctrinated—so brainwashed—that deprogramming them would be a challenge in and of itself. The added challenge was that, even among our close friends, it was difficult to know who to trust. "What if our friends who were still in NXIVM were spying on us? Could they be trusted?" We had to be careful, since we had no idea what they would do with the collateral. To our knowledge, all they knew was there was a group of defectors who were having some issues.

*

I handed over my folder, containing the collateral I collected, to Mark, as evidence this time, so that he could present it to the FBI. I felt that I had done my part, so I departed for Hawaii, ready for a new chapter, to be far away from The Vow and to be where I wanted to be this entire time. I had already jumped from Albany, where I'd never been, and was about to jump to Hawaii, where I had visited only once before. My first trip to Hawaii completely changed my life. It's the first place that ever felt like home to me. When I returned to LA, my goal was to go back to Hawaii for an extended amount of time. Shortly after that, I ended up at the NXIVM presentation. Instead of spending the money I saved to go back to Hawaii, I spent my savings on ESP. I knew about two people in Hawaii, and when I showed up, I had no money; just had to tap in to find my way and make things work. I sold all my things and bought a one-way ticket to Maui. "God lives in Maui," I told myself.

My heart exploded when I flew over the island. It felt like a relief, as if I was coming home, specifically to Maui. I felt the happiness surge in my heart. It was a new beginning and a new life. Waiting at the airport for my friend to pick me up, the air was warm and had a certain floral, salty ocean smell. I hopped in my friend's truck and realized: "I am *here*. I made it." I was broke, with a couple hundred dollars in my account, and I didn't know what I was going to do. But none of that mattered—I knew I was where I was meant to be.

My friend offered to let me stay at his place for a few weeks, where I had some space to process. My plan started to unfold slowly when I arrived. Despite being a risk-taker, I needed time to feel my way around. Over the first couple of days, I spent time alone and was searching. I found a coffee shop first, and then slowly began to find a rhythm. "The islands will show you where you need to go," my friend told me. He continued, "I knew you would be back here—one way or another. You belong here." That's how the islands work: if someone is not meant to be there, the islands will kick you off. The same thing goes the other way. The island knows. The island dictates whether you fit in or not. Some people move to Hawaii and think they just landed in paradise—until things start to fall apart, they get arrested, they lose their job, lose their house—and the islands reject them. Especially those who have no intention of giving back to the *aina* (the land). On the flip side, if it's meant to work out, things will align for you.

When I was growing up, I moved around a lot and needed to take in new surroundings. Being naturally curious, I was always up for an adventure, and I loved to be immersed in things. Being at a coffee shop nearby meant I could write and contemplate, but also plan my next steps away from the noise. I was not trying to tune out my experience with NXIVM, but rather to process emotions and thoughts at the same time. I spent hours journaling and going over my experience. This was exactly where I wanted to be. I was open to anything.

However, being open can be a double-edged sword. Being open and vulnerable to anything made it possible for me to have a fulfilling life. But, on the other hand, without boundaries and discernment, being open and vulnerable hurt me. Still, I left the lines of communication open to people from NXIVM. Even though I was leaving the past behind and moving forward, there were still people I cared about and was willing to put myself on the line for to help them. People in Albany reached out to me to ask what was happening. "Listen," I said, "I am trusting you right now. It's dangerous for me." Because I cared about them, I told them my story, hoping that it would inspire them to leave Albany and NXIVM altogether. I let go of things that I didn't really need. This was an entirely different Jess than the person I was in Albany. I repeatedly cracked open my human shell to better understand who I was and who I was about to become. Hawaii was the place that would allow me to do the deep healing work that I needed to pursue. I also met my *ohana* there. My experience in Hawaii was literally the opposite of my previously shallow and jaded LA life.

People were genuinely friendly, caring, and respectful. No one wanted anything from me, and people were so kind and helpful—out of the pure goodness of their hearts. I finally felt like I had met my people. The *aloha* spirit is something so real and something I personally believe is the microcosm of the macrocosm of what's possible in the world. For instance, if we went to visit one of my friends who has children, who you've never met before, my friend would say, "Say hi to your auntie" (or to your uncle). It's the belief that we're one family—that is, humanity is one family. Living in Hawaii allowed me to be able to operate from my heart space every day. I felt safe to be myself, my true self, and was surrounded by other people living from that same space. Hawaii will always be home to me, and I am beyond grateful to have had the honor of being there, especially during that time.

*

Everything sped into motion when *The New York Times*' article came out. The *Times*' exposé about women getting branded made waves. One afternoon, my lawyer called me to tell me the FBI wanted to talk. I was one of the first people the FBI talked to. Originally, since I was not branded, nor did I complete my special assignment, I figured that my testimony would not be *that* critical. After all, "there are women who had suffered far worse than I," I thought. However, it turned out that my testimony was so important that two FBI agents (Mike and Charlie) turned up in Hawaii, having flown from New York, just to meet with me.

The agents stayed for a total of 48 hours. They looked at me with curiosity; I could not tell at the time whether I was the one under the microscope, or who I was signing up to eliminate. The agents told me to expect to receive a call with orders to pack my bags. I was beginning a journey with them, and I realized soon I would be spending a lot of time in New York.

After meeting the FBI agents, I spent a year in Hawaii. But I knew that New York was going to be in my foreseeable future. I moved back to LA in order to make it easier to commute to New York: a five-hour flight one way from LA, versus a ten-hour flight from Hawaii to JFK. It was time for that adventure to come to an end, so that I could start my next mission. Things rapidly changed after Keith fled to Mexico with Marianna, the mother of his newborn child, as well as a handful of first-line slaves including Allison. Keith also had connections to affluent families in Mexico, including a close relationship with Emiliano Salinas, the son of the former President of Mexico, Carlos Salinas. The FBI arrested Keith in a private, gated, upscale villa where he thought he could hide. I learned that the indictment itself had been served with my own personal contributions dotted onto it. There were only two Jane Does on the indictment: I was one of them.

Hindsight Is 20/20

For years, I had the life of the quintessential LA "hot girl." In August 2016, I took my first ESP intensive—I put my foot on the gas pedal and, to this day, I haven't lifted it off. Since then, I've wanted to write about the NXIVM experience—about Keith, Allison, and about India and the trial—as well as the others who were caught up in NXIVM, just before the ship sank. Writing this book only came to me when I stepped back to realize that this life is crazy. This happened while I was sitting on the floor in my new apartment—my first apartment since leaving Albany. It was an empty room, as the only belongings I had were a couple suitcases filled with my clothes and personal keepsakes. I had been bouncing around LA until I finally settled down and started over. I ordered a mattress but no bed frame, which is where I sat to take it all in.

I listened to Jhene Aiko, who calmed my nerves with her lilting voice, but also stirred up untapped feelings, which somehow brought tears to the surface. Some days it felt like so much—too much. But I knew even on my weakest day, I could lead an army, and on my strongest day there still lived the little girl inside me that had enough.

I find myself caressing my inner palms over and over again, which quickly takes me into a memory of the memories I've had, most recent of which, are the life lessons. Life is really nothing more than an uninterrupted lesson—one after another. The lessons I've had I believe have always been blessings, but these kinds of blessings come with a price, one I was always destined to bear.

Other times, the weight of the world, and the 'knowing,' makes me feel helpless. If it wasn't for the feeling of truth deep inside me and witnessing miracles, I don't know if I could believe what I believe. This world is so full of pain, suffering, and darkness. We're literally born into a system of oppression, brainwashed by the media and prescribed emotional repression from society. I didn't always know what I know now. The chains weren't visible; instead, they were shiny and fulfilled my materialistic desires. How was I to know—to see what's really going on in the world and the degree of harm being done to humanity? All I know is that I was born to fight. The warrior blood runs deep through my many ancestors.

Sometimes I just want to rest, like a soldier wounded in battle. Some rest. Some peace. The truth is we're not free until we're all free, which is why I fight for the freedom of others, but the first person to be unchained must be myself. Only in my own liberation can I be an example and inspiration of how others can do it themselves. I'm not saying I have all the answers, but I do have some. I've walked many paths and turned in many directions. I just pray that my experiences and story will help even just one person believe in themselves and know that they deserve the Love and Life that they want. I never said it would be easy, but it is an absolute possibility and birthright.

What happens when I'm alone? In the dark? Last night, I almost had to sleep with the light on. I kept having this looming fear, this vision of a man attacking me, trying to kill me. It doesn't help that I am extremely empathic and watched the *Ted Bundy* Netflix movie not that long ago. This type of fear is not something new. Its presence comes in waves. I don't believe there is only one trigger for it.

I think that most women have this thought or fear cross their minds at least one time in their lives. We, as women, have been oppressed and are the target of physical violence, rape, molestation, emotional abuse, and manipulation. Our greatest predators have been men. The Divine Feminine has been bruised, battered, and left for dead; just look at the desolation Mother Earth has been experiencing. We all have played a part in this, as we have neglected to empower ourselves.

Most of us have not been taught the truth of our power. Or how to wield it.

"Why did I end up in ESP?" I think. My main reasons for seeking out ESP, and the road of personal development, is because I am a seeker, looking for the deeper truths and meanings of life. It's because I was severely damaged and traumatized in my childhood, which festered into my own self destruction and soul annihilation leading into my adulthood. After years of repeating painful patterns and being sick and tired of feeling like shit, I started looking inward.

I've always been tapped into higher planes of consciousness since I was a child, but as soon as my mom chose a life of drugs and abandoned me and my siblings, it started placing layers of pain and dysfunction onto my truth. In my core, I have always been in my light, but I didn't know it. I also dimmed my light, and gave it away to people who didn't deserve it. I allowed myself to be disregarded and disrespected, because that's how I interpreted my mother leaving me. As a child I didn't have the ability to comprehend and understand that my mom had her own demons that she was facing and was incapable of being a mother. I felt her disregard for me meant that I wasn't worthy of love. Pain and loss became my base point, and my entire understanding of what love was.

*

After NXVIM, I resolved to do exactly the opposite of what my experience had been. In fact, it was the catalyst for me to dive into my deepest work to get me to where I am now. It was my initiation from the Universe to truly live in my purpose. Dividing my time between healing, transformation, and devoting myself to Spirit in order to help others.

The case against NXIVM was entitled *UNITED STATES OF AMERICA v. KEITH RANIERE, also known as "The Vanguard."* The arrest warrant alleged NXIVM committed knowing or intentional "commercial sex acts," or sex trafficking, through threats of force and coercion. The government described NXIVM's activities with a high level of detail, despite the levels of secrecy, non-disclosure agreements, and attempts to keep things about NXIVM from the public. Other aspects of NXIVM were widely known, such as "Vanguard Week," which was a celebration of Keith Raniere in upstate New York during the month of August for his birthday.

When the trial started, I couldn't help but read all the awful details of what that man has done. Some days I felt heroic, but most days it was in the way back part of my mind. "Who am I? What is this? This is pretty crazy, right?" My life has been a rollercoaster. Unorthodox would be an understatement. Sometimes I feel like I'm not even here, like nothing is even real.

In November 2018, before the trial began, I was walking in LA on Beverly Boulevard, when I was hit by a car in the middle of a crosswalk. I was on my way to meet a friend for dinner. The driver didn't see me. I tore both my MCL and ACL and, as a result, couldn't work my normal jobs, exercise, or do yoga for a year. I became extremely depressed. It was my "Golem" stage (I called it) because I only wore a giant green hoodie and refused to leave my cave (friend's apartment) or see friends. When I finally got fitted for a brace, I limped around an upscale hotel in Beverly Hills where I was hired to serve demanding guests for 10-plus hour shifts—unable to use my looks and charm, I couldn't wear sexy outfits and make money by just being cute, like my bottle service days. Most days felt unbearable, but I am grateful for this experience because it fortified me.

Just before I was hit in the crosswalk, I had been in Paris, starring in my own short film that I executive produced. The film was an adaptation based on one of my poems, called *gLOVEs*. I went from acting as the lead in my film, to getting hit by a car—it was another reminder of how unpredictable life is. When my friends found out about the accident, they said, "This could only happen to *you*." The combination of intense and wild events that I've gone through is utterly characteristic of my life. My injury humbled me, a sort of rebirth that led me through another lesson of rebuilding, facing adversity, and getting back up.

After the accident, I found myself entering a new tournament, traveling to and from New York, beginning my preparation for the trial. The Assistant District Attorney prosecuting the case with the FBI asked me frankly, "Who do you think the bad guys are?" There had been no mention to that point of good and bad, but could there really be any doubt about it? When the trial began, I took the stand for two days. These were heated segments. The first day lasted about 30 minutes, and the second day, about 45 minutes, which were animated and detailed. It was like a boxing match between me and the defense attorney. I was Muhammed Ali. I was on fire. "Move like a butterfly, sting like a bee."

The dimwitted defense attorney tried tirelessly to defame my character, but ended up shuffling back to his seat, frantically searching for papers and flustered by my testimony. I confronted his tiny eyes with a fearless smile. All I was doing was telling the truth. When you're living in your truth, there's nothing that can touch you.

*

Spirit sent me in with a job to do, which was to help take NXIVM down, to learn my own lessons and heal myself along the way. My final duty in the matter was to give my victim impact statement for Allison Mack's sentencing in person. This is what I said:

> Your Honor, I've traveled across the country and spent the last of my unemployment just to be here to make sure my voice was present, heard and accounted for, not just for me but for all my sisters who are unable to be here today, for all of Allison's victims who do not have a voice, to not only warn you and the rest of the world but to also shine light on the truth of who Allison Mack truly is.
>
> Allison Mack is a predator and an evil human being, a danger to society with no care, remorse or empathy for her victims.
>
> When I woke up one morning to an article about her asking for no jail time because she turned her life around, I was horrified. I wanted to scream to the top of my lungs. I was triggered back into a memory of a real life nightmare she had already put me through.
>
> Your Honor, my name is Jessica Joan. Through this case, you've known me as Witness Jay. You heard my story and all the horrors I've had to endure growing up, from being raped, molested, to being abandoned by my mother as a small child, and with all of that

combined, Allison Mack and Keith Raniere are the most evil monsters I've ever met.

I met Allison on my first trip to Albany. She was a Proctor leading my group during the ESP intensive. From the moment I met her, she made me feel like she was a kind, loving and deeply empathetic person. The way she would look into my eyes would make me feel seen, like she really cared.

She felt like the big sister I wish I had. Even at the very beginning of joining The Vow, she would tell me how she'd always be there to look after and protect me. Allison knew all the right things to say in order to lure me in.

Once I joined The Vow and learned that she was my Grand Master, she admitted that she was intentionally leading my group in order to find out who I was. So, from the very beginning, she was probing into my psyche learning what made me tick, what drove me and also my deepest vulnerabilities.

Allison is very clear and calculated in the moves she makes, just like when she would randomly ask me how I felt about Keith, what did I think about him, or when she told me that seduction and sexual power isn't bad if it is used for good. The whole time she had been playing me and, worst of all, grooming me into becoming a sex slave for her beloved Keith Raniere.

Allison maliciously gave me—a survivor of rape and sexual assault—a special assignment, an honor and privilege to seduce Keith and have him take a naked picture of me to prove I did it. And when I pushed back confused, I asked if Keith knew about The Vow. She blatantly lied and said that doing this assignment would get rid of all my issues around being sexually abused.

This demon of a woman literally tried to use my pain, suffering and traumas against me to be abused by another monster. She intended and tried to hurt the little girl inside of me yet again, the little girl that she watched cry her eyes out night after night reliving these traumas.

Let me be very clear, she ended the phone call with a sinister: "And I give you permission to enjoy it."

So, when she was on house arrest hanging with her family, taking Berkeley Women's Studies courses online and enjoying the Orange County sunshine and sipping lattes and putting on lip gloss with her friends, her victims were left hiding in the dark corners of their homes reliving the fear, silence and horror that Allison put us through.

She worked her way into my heart. She made me believe that she would do anything for me but the truth is, she sought me out like a predator stalking their prey, another little lamb for her to slaughter.

She saw the little Jess inside of me and exploited her. She stabbed her and watched her bleed out.

I could blame myself for falling for it, but the truth is I was so desperately needing to feel loved, I felt so alone. Everyone in my life had left me in the dust and I just wanted to feel like I mattered, that someone cared about me.

Allison will never know and feel the ramifications of her actions. She's grown up in a pretty and privileged life, always protected, never knowing the consequences of her actions. She plays the victim so well. She can blame Keith all she wants, but she is a monster cut from the same cloth.

The fact of the matter is she gained much pleasure out of other people's pain, myself included. I saw the evil glimmer in her eyes and the sick sadistic smile on her face whenever she would punish us. She took great pride and joy knowing she had total control, having blackmail to make us do whatever she wanted. She used fear to intimidate and coerce her supposed sisters to do things against our will.

I truly believe there aren't enough years in the rest of her lifetime to even begin to undo the harm, pain and suffering she has caused me and the rest of her victims.

If I would have gone through with her attempt to sex traffic me, I know I wouldn't be able to stand here in front of you today. And to think I'm one of the lucky ones. I don't have to walk around with a permanent brand in my pelvic region, none of the beautiful symbols representing the elements that she claimed but of her and Keith's initials; women mutilated and branded like cattle for her to forever have power and dominion over them with that symbol burned onto their bodies.

Again, I stand here not only for myself but for all the other countless victims unable to be present today and the friends, families and loved ones forever affected by Allison's actions. Her poison does not only affect the victims and loved ones, but it also bleeds into future generations.

I repeat this from the depths of my heart: Allison Mack is an evil sociopath, a menace to society and a danger to innocent beings. She may put on a good show, but don't let her fool you. I know exactly who she is. She's the Ghislaine Maxwell to Keith's Jeffrey Epstein, and I just pray that she gets what she deserves.

Allison, I thought I was going to be angry standing here looking you face-to-face, but I'm just sad, I'm sad because you had everything and it wasn't enough. I had nothing and you tried to break me and you tried to dim my light. You imprisoned us but by the grace of God, we are free and now it's your turn to be imprisoned and feel as alone and broken as we once did. Only then can you begin to reflect on
your actions and darkness in hopes that one day you see the light, then maybe, just maybe you can be free too.

Your Honor, I have complete trust and faith in your empathy, discernment and understanding. I believe you will bring justice to myself and all the other victims of Allison Mack. Thank you for your time.

There's a deep stirring in my soul when I think about forgiving Allison and the others in NXIVM for what they did. There are two parts, really: do I forgive myself for being in that situation? I have largely accepted and absolved myself of any guilt or regret for having to go through that experience. The second part, however, is understanding the character of the people involved in NXIVM. When I view the spirit of those who harmed me, I can see the lost souls, which made them easy prey for evil to permeate through them. With Allison, it's not only that she harmed me and other people, but the fact that she does not necessarily care or have any real remorse. That's part of the reason why I was motivated to give my victim impact statement. A message must be delivered because people who perform evil acts get away with things every day. My anger is not necessarily about an inability to forgive, but it is about the injustice that exists when people perpetuate evil and go unpunished.

The emotional abuse that was inflicted had a sinister quality to it. Allison would talk down to us, bring up insecurities she was aware of, berate us, and then try to smooth it over with love-bombing. There was exploitation of trust built through the process. This was textbook emotional manipulation: disrespect, guilt-tripping, gaslighting, and leveraging my emotions against me. Towards the end, Allison said that I was one of the only people who stood up to her and that her tactics did not work on me.

My anger towards Allison was only harming myself; by holding onto the hot stone, I was burning myself. I returned to my Spirit and Creator. There is light within us all when we're born. Allison was once filled with light, only to have lost it, which is what enabled her to create so much destruction. Someone filled with love would not do these things. Tapping into the "little Allison" allowed me to both feel empathy and to process my own feelings—to transmute my anger and to turn it into something positive. My anger was eating away at my light, which is exactly what the evil opposition wants, so in going into a space of love and forgiveness, I was able to heal myself and forgive Allison and the other lost souls, because ultimately, I know that love defeats evil. And love always wins.

*

As this story ends, a new chapter unfolds. This has been one hell of a ride, and I still haven't taken my foot off the gas pedal. I am so grateful to my readers, those of you who have joined me on this journey, for reading my story—this book is for you. My purpose in sharing everything inside is to help people. Writing this book has helped me heal tremendously and freed me to the point where I am Untouchable. Now, for the first time, I am finally living and walking from an empowered place, from my truth and from who I really am. I pray that my story helps you to know that you can go through anything and still come out smiling. Life is worth fighting for. I am very excited for what's next. I have so many stories, so much art, and even other books inside of me that I can't wait to share with the world. I am living in my purpose—to help others, to help empower women especially, and to protect children. This is just the beginning . . .

and I want you to know that I love you.

Nine Steps of Transmutation

These are the nine steps I've taken to transform my life, as well as the principles that I live by. These steps I've found to be the most important tools I've learned on my journey of self-love and healing. I've learned these tools, and how to apply them, through many aspects of my life from practitioners, teachers, and guides, to accidents, retreats, reading books and articles, as well as my own personal experience, and divine intervention.

In my experience, what I believe to be the foundation of transmutation is truth. Only in being honest with yourself, and having a full, clear picture of your life, can you have the ability to change your life into what you want it to be. "Trauma is not your fault, but healing is your responsibility." My hope and dream are for these steps, or even just one of them, to help you heal something that's been on your heart—and to give you the freedom for you to experience inner peace. I'm a huge believer of journaling and writing things down, especially when it comes to manifesting. All of the nine steps are set with the intention of journaling your awareness's and self-reflections.

1. <u>Your Body Is Your Temple</u>

My first step to my awakening was through detoxing my body. Growing up, and not having money, we ate a lot of fast food and things that were just not healthy. It wasn't until I started doing cleanses and colonics that I really started to open and elevate energetically. The Universe is always sending us messages. But it takes clarity and self-awareness to be able to receive and decipher these messages, which is why treating your body as a temple is of the utmost importance.

If you think of yourself as a radio, and you need to send and receive signals, then it's important to be tuned to the right station. But if you're clogged up with bad food, drugs, alcohol, trauma, and negative patterns, it makes the signal unclear—it clogs up the air space. The signal is weak. Your body has trillions of cells that are all their own tiny universes—full of information and wisdom. Our body is here to protect our insides, to make sure we're healthy and happy.

In our modern world, and society at large, there are so many things that work against us. From poison in the air and water, to being fed food that's not even really food, to even the way the media makes us feel that we're inadequate, like we're somehow less than. The fact is that Spirit already made us perfect.

What you're consuming—what you eat, who you listen to, what you watch—will create and determine the quality of your lifestyle and mindset. Eating healthy can be expensive, but it's also about where you place your value. Perhaps you go out for coffee, or partying, or prioritizing other things besides their health. It's all about what you prioritize. If you're a billionaire, but you're sick and unwell, the money is irrelevant. I personally choose to eat a certain way because that's my health insurance. In that way, I focus on preventative and holistic healing, instead of waiting to become sick and finding a cure-all remedy, which doesn't necessarily cure anything, but tends to simply suppress the underlying symptoms.

When you treat your body with love and care, it can do more for you. For a long time, I struggled with eating disorders and being hyper-judgmental and critical of my body. It took getting into an accident, literally my body being hit by a car, in order for me to learn how to appreciate my body as it is. I now understand how hard it works to protect me, whereas before I was constantly poking and prodding at my body to look a certain way. My injury really showed me the path to appreciating and loving my body and myself.

Internal traumas and unaddressed issues can also create manifestations of dis-ease, illness, pains and other physical issues. These are signals our body is trying to communicate to us that something isn't right. We currently live in a society that breeds stress through broken systems of oppression, images of success through winning at a fake rat race and pitting us against each other until we go way beyond the point of exhaustion, left with no time for ourselves let alone those we love and care for There is no gold medal you win by simply being busy. In fact one of the acts of rebellion and acts of self-love is rest. Rest is a birthright, and our bodies require this love and time to reintegrate all the emotional, mental, spiritual and physical experiences we go through.

We are not robots and we've been taught that operating like one will lead us to happiness and freedom. We've been lied to. With that being said "being healthy" can also be a form of addiction and create more harm. I've had to learn this the hard way, more times than once. The key here is balance. I make decisions and take actions in alignment with my purpose, but as a dear friend taught me "it's not a straight jacket." That way I'm fully loving myself and honoring all my needs. Without judgement, but with clarity, love and discernment. Nurture your body, care for your temple and it will bless you back tenfold.

I invite you to take the time, to pause, to take a breath and just sit with your hands on your heart and listen to what your body is trying to tell you.

2.   Clarity: What Do You Want?

If you don't know what you want, you won't know where you're going. It's like being a ship at sea with no sails pointing you in any direction. Just floating in the middle of the ocean. There is nothing wrong with that as everyone is on their own journey and own timing. Some enjoy going with the flow, but if you want to manifest a certain life, it's imperative you know what you want. Most people don't actually know what they want. They think what they want is what society has told them, what their friends have told them, their parents, or even social media for that matter.

We have a bunch of people chasing a bunch of different things that, at their core, they don't even really care about. This is why really knowing what you want is so important. If you don't know what you want, life is just going to point you into whatever direction the wind takes you. If you want to achieve something, and you have goals and dreams, you need to know exactly what you want. You don't necessarily need to know how, but you need to know what and you need to know why. When you have clarity of mind and clarity in your heart, there isn't anything you can't achieve. But when you have distractions and are afraid of actually knowing what it is that you want, it only holds you back.

Sitting alone with yourself is some of the most important work you'll ever do. To really ask the questions about: what would make you happy in life? what is your heart's true desire? What does your dream life look like? Only you know what that is. No one is going to tell you. Whenever I need clarity on a subject, I set myself up in the perfect environment: no distractions, a clean space, and I get an unlined notebook and a blue-ink pen, and I sit, I think, I feel, and I envision. I ask myself: "What do I want? What would make me happy?" These are general questions I have when I think about my life, but there's also specific questions that I ask myself when I have a certain goal in mind. Let's use moving to a new home as an example.

I visualize myself in this new home; I focus on the feeling of being there. I focus on the non-negotiables, how much I want to pay, how many bedrooms, what is the lighting like, what area—and for me personally, I need to have a bathtub (because taking Epsom salt baths recharge me and are a necessary part of my well-being). You need to think about, feel, and visualize the things that will make you happy and bring you joy. Don't think about: "Oh, I can't have that," or "That's too much." It doesn't cost you anything to be creative and use your imagination, and then actually believe that you deserve to feel that way. However due to conditioning from the limiting beliefs imposed by others, the society, media and even generational and ancestral trauma, getting to the core of our desires may take some unmasking. You may be chasing this idea that having a corporate job, so you can have the luxury car and designer clothes will make you happy, when all you want to do is live in a cabin off grid tending to your garden. Or for my fellow Filipinos, being a nurse or doctor because that's what your parents expect of you, but all you want is to be a comedian, break-dancer, painter. It doesn't matter what it is, as long as it's yours.

I invite you to ask yourself what truly brings you joy and lights you up inside, then visualize yourself living your life as that.

3.   Get Comfortable with Discomfort (Personal Inventory)

No one's perfect. Everyone's got at least one skeleton, if not many, in their closet. Just know that. Take out a notebook and a pen. Now is the time to take personal inventory and look at all your ugly parts. Unless you're a narcissist, you know there are some things you do that can use some improvement. If you're lucky enough, you have people in your life who care enough about you and are willing to tell you about these uncomfortable truths. Now is the time for total honesty with yourself; now is the time to write down all the negative behaviors, and things that you do that are not in alignment with your favorite version of yourself.

No one is here to judge you or say you're a bad person. But this is the time to elevate, grow, and transform into the version of yourself that you want and know you can be. It doesn't happen overnight because it doesn't happen unless you do the work. So, ta-da, there it is: total, brutal honesty. I used to be very entitled—I didn't even realize this because I had such a hard life, and a standard about how I expected people to be. But in the same token, I was afforded a lot of privileges because of how I look, which I didn't take account for.

I felt like the world owed me things. I had very little compassion for others. Growing up in LA, being surrounded by a bunch of yes-people, I couldn't recognize my behavior until my little sister would tell me I was being a certain way. I wouldn't listen to her; only one person's voice wouldn't make a difference. It wasn't until my ex-boyfriend really pointed it out for me that I really started to wake up and see how I was behaving, and that it was a character trait I didn't want to imbue.

So, it took a lot of work for me to call myself out and take a pause. I didn't change this behavior overnight but, as soon as I became aware of it, and really started digging deeper, and felt the burn of that behavior, did I start to change it. Are there some things that I feel entitled to still? Sure, it's not a complete detriment. But I am no longer entitled and self-righteous in the way that I used to be. Sometimes it's O.K. to feel entitled to things, particularly so you don't get taken advantage of. Think of personal inventory as a "pros and cons" list for yourself. Start by embracing the things you love about yourself: your kindness, care, generosity, attentiveness, etc. Now I want you to look at those qualities and find out the intention and reason behind these behaviors. Of course, it's core is probably rooted in your heart and being a good natured person. But I want you to dissect yourself and see if these behaviors ever led to your feelings being hurt when an expectation wasn't met. Or if your behaviors were fueled out of survival, people pleasing or even a self-defense mechanism. There is nothing wrong with the reason, it's just important to become aware of it. To strip down ourselves and see the truth of our being so we can move forward in full control of ourselves and not become slaves to our emotions or traumas.

Now I want you to do the same with your "cons" list. Are you short tempered, do you close off when you start to get vulnerable, do you suppress your feelings, maybe passive aggressive? I used to be passive aggressive. I didn't know how to express my truth in a healthy way. I was severely repressed. I didn't express my true feelings when someone hurt them. I would either just take the pain and bottle it up (poetry helped me express myself) or I would simply cut off the person or run away from the thing that was making me feel uncomfortable. It wasn't until a friend of mine literally forced me to express my feelings. When I would get upset with her, I would just be silent or say something mean in a passive way. She said she would have rather I yelled at her for being a jerk, instead of silently bottling up my anger. I finally let out my feelings and it felt so good. It was relieving. Then I started to unpack the passive aggressiveness and correlate it back to when I wanted to share my feelings with my mother, and she cut me off. I discovered that this is when my throat chakra closed and created this limitation in my expression. After getting to the root of this trauma-based behavior, I was able to transmute the energy. Now it is a huge part of my being to express my truth and my feelings. I literally feel sick in my body if I try to hold back my truth.

I invite you to be completely honest and raw with yourself. I also invite you to ask your closest confidants whom you trust, and you know only have your best interest in mind and ask them what are some qualities you possess that are working against you becoming your best self. Everyone has an opinion, and some may tell you things that are hard to hear. You will be able to identify it as truth if what they say resonates with you or if you feel a trigger. Underneath the trigger is a wound. We often times judge others, ourselves or project our pain without realizing it. Everyone and everything is just a mirror. A mirror for us to look deeper within ourselves, to see the parts of ourselves we've forgotten, neglected or even been hating. At the end of the day, we're all connected as a collective consciousness and we're not well until we're all well.

4. Personal Responsibility vs. Victim Mentality

For trauma and abuse to happen, there must be an oppressor and a victim. This is a fact. However, there is a huge difference between being victimized and playing the victim. Maybe we're all guilty of playing the victim, at some point in life, either big or small. For a lot of people who have been abused, it can be hard to decipher between being present with one's pain versus enacting the pain over and over.

When you take ownership of your pain and trauma, you're able to empower yourself—and not let that pain and trauma run your life. But, when you play the victim, and adopt the victim mentality, you're disempowered and are willingly giving control of your life to external factors. Sometimes it feels good to play the victim, to get attention, to be heard and seen, but ultimately, the only person you're hurting is yourself.

When we don't heal our trauma, we allow these negative patterns to play out in our life and effect everyone around us. Taking personal responsibility in our life not only gives us power but is also our responsibility to our community and the world at large. When you're living the same story repeatedly, you don't evolve past the pain and trauma in your story. You can't move forward or ever be truly happy. Victim mentality always puts you in a place of vulnerability because you are relying on someone or something outside of yourself to make your situation better. No one's going to save you. I am often asked how have I been able to persevere in spite of traumatic childhood and chaotic life challenges. My answer at its core, "I didn't have a choice." Sure, of course there was always an alternative route where I didn't empower myself and allowed my past to dictate my future. There were plenty of times and years that went by with me blaming my mother for abandoning me or my uncle for sexually abusing me, for causing me insurmountable pain and suffering. But that's just it, I took personal responsibility for myself and creating the future I want and deserve. I wasn't going to allow those experiences hinder me, instead I used it as fuel by overcoming and facing it all. A process that still occurs, because the healing gets deeper and doing the work just allows the recovery time to be quicker.

I invite you to see the places where you place blame on others, your boss, your parents, society and reframe the blame into asking yourself "What can I do change this?" We are all capable of so much for than we realize, especially when we don't wait for someone else to fix our problems, but instead roll up our sleeves and do whatever it takes.

5. <u>Course Correct (Let Go, Shed, Elevate)</u>

Life is about living. Going after things. Making memories. Following your path. Or getting into a bunch of different adventures; there's right or wrong way, if you're being curious, exploring, and just doing. However, along these paths of adventures, sometimes we go down the wrong road. And that's O.K. Even though that road may feel wrong, in the grand scheme of things, there was something to be learned there. I don't believe in regrets. I believe that we would do better if we knew better.

Which brings us to "course correct." It's exactly like it sounds. Like a ship on the water, headed in a certain direction that's a little 'off' from its direction. We don't freak out. We just recalibrate and get back on track. This is exactly what I did with the NXIVM situation. I thought I was headed in the right direction; I thought that was where I was supposed to be going—and in the big picture, I was. Not just because of the personal lessons, but also because of the people that received justice from that situation because of me being there and helping take it down.

As soon as I got my "special assignment," I had to course correct. I came up with a plan, then figured out the steps I needed to take to make the plan successful, and then I executed those steps. So, what turned into a bad situation, ended up being very liberating, full of lessons, and a blessing to many. So, don't beat yourself up, or feel stupid—it's O.K. to make mistakes. It's O.K. to end up in weird situations, especially if you course correct. That experience gives you the wisdom and knowledge to do better in the future.

There is no perfect way. I truly believe we are each on our own personal journey, living in our own divine timing and that everything happens for a reason. Something I'm so grateful that life has taught me is that it's okay to fall on my face, time heals, and I can always get back up again. I could have allowed my fear of my collateral being released or embarrassment in falling into a cult keep me silent. Instead, I used the wisdom and fire inside me to turn this unfortunate event into something empowering. I got myself out of that situation before it got worse, I did what I needed to do to protect myself and I helped the FBI take down some seriously evil individuals. And now I'm getting to share my experience to help others. I wouldn't have had it any other way. The way I live is I keep the ship moving with my destination in my mind's eye. I welcome the adventure while also knowing when to change gears and even take a pit stop, if necessary. I just don't quit.

I invite you to assess your own ship of your life and see if there are any areas that need some course correcting or simply keep this lesson in you back pocket should it need to be visited in the future. You are the captain of your ship, with your Higher Self leading the way.

6.   Forgive Yourself and Others

The act of forgiveness is imperative for our healing and to attaining true "self-love." When we carry judgement, pain, shame, guilt and anger for all the harm we've been caused, consciously or unconsciously we project that onto others. We carry an energetic frequency of self-hatred which reflects onto our experience. There are many people in my life that have hurt me and caused me great pain—who have violated my body and have broken my heart.

I would not have been able to endure all the pain that I have if I did not have the ability to forgive. With every cut, there's a weight that's added to your soul and onto your heart. If you don't forgive and allow these things to heal, you walk around carrying all this weight. It takes away from your light, your happiness, your joy—and for some people, their reason for living. I am grateful for the pain I've experienced, because it has given me depth. Some of the deepest waters that I would have drowned in had I not been able to forgive. Forgiveness has given me the ability to swim. The ability to enjoy the rainbows after a storm. Forgiveness is not always easy, especially when it comes to forgiving ourselves. During my "Party Jess" days I put myself in compromising situations, some that could have been potentially very dangerous to my well-being. I was reckless and careless with myself, drinking excessively and partaking in extracurricular activities until the sun came up. I was poisoning my body, damaging my spirit and creating more heartbreak for myself and others.

Early on in my healing journey I just dismissed that old version of myself. I tried to hide and forget about her, but that version of myself represented a very important part of me. She was the one who suffered from immense hurt, spawn from my traumatized and abandoned inner child. She was the version of me who learned to survive and find ways to cope and enjoy life while internally suffering to the point of no longer wanting to exist. For so long I put so much guilt, shame and blame on her. Rejecting this part of myself that already felt unloved and rejected. Now here I am able to have so much love and compassion for her, for me, my inner child for everything I have endured and gone through to be the version of myself that I am so proud of. This didn't happen overnight. So many sleepless nights, tear-soaked journals, to being sick to my stomach uncomfortable looking at myself in the mirror and saying "I am amazing" over and over bawling, because I realized how much I hated myself. Until one day it didn't hurt anymore when I did my mirror work. I now gladly scream to the top of my lungs how incredible I am. No longer am I playing small or not shining my light, because I earned this joy right here. I've danced with the devil and clawed my way out of hell to love myself. And you can too.

The act of forgiveness is so important—because forgiveness is for you. Forgiveness is for your freedom; freedom from the pain that others have caused you, and that you have caused yourself. Forgiveness gives you your power back. It's the lifeblood for your heart to continue to love. And love is everything.

I invite you to do some mirror work on your own. You can start with a simple affirmation "I love you." "I'm sorry." "I'm beautiful." or anything else you want to say to yourself or new belief you want to engrain. Now the trick is to look deep into your eyes as you say the affirmation to yourself. At first it might feel strange or uncomfortable, but just keep going.

7.   Service Is an Act of Self-Love

Spirit is in service to us all. To be alive is a blessing. The greatest gift we can give in this life is to be of service to others. To be able to be of service, and to give, is to show that you have more than enough. That you are abundant and prosperous. There is no other feeling like giving from your heart—to help someone else in need, and to be able to uplift someone's spirit.

When you think about being in service to others and think about the time that someone has helped you, and how that made you feel, that's the same feeling you're giving to someone else when you're in service to others. It doesn't cost anything to be kind. Offering a helping hand goes farther than you'll ever know. To love others is to love yourself. Because we're all connected, an act of kindness to someone else is ultimately an act of kindness towards yourself. Love is abundant and the most powerful thing in the world. So, when you're being of service and giving love, you're literally making the world a better place. And you get to live in this better place.

Now there are caveats to this. Ones that I, again, had to learn the hard way. Being a heart centered human being is a gift, a blessing, but can also be a liability. I would never change the nature of my heart, for she is pure and true. However, my heart's ever-loving nature and desire to help others has also put me in positions that ended up with me compromising myself. One of the greatest lessons I learned from my NXIVM experience was "discernment." Living life from a selfless and caring lens is beautiful and truly rare. This is the essence of the angelic realm. It is a quality that sets people apart. It's easy to be selfish, self-motivated, self-focused, but to sacrifice, to care for others, that's where the magic lives.

169

However, this selflessness unchecked can lead you to be taken advantage of or leave you with an empty cup. There is a balance with self-love and being of service. One of the ways I live by, is that I only pour when my cup is overflowing. I don't pour from my reserves, let alone an empty cup. I used to pour from my reserves and even when my cup was empty, because even when I had nothing, the love in my heart just wanted to keep giving. Now, yes this may seem admirable, which in a way that is an admirable quality, but when one operates from that space as a constant that becomes abuse and neglect of the self. Intention is everything, so just check in with yourself and really feel why you are wanting to give. Is it a stirring from your heart, is it the right thing to do, or is it just something you feel obligated to do. The magic that comes from giving is in the energy of the giving. Give with love or just take a pause and evaluate your intention. Be that beautiful, giving, caring self and shine that light. Care for others, just make sure you're pouring that love into yourself as well.

I invite you to pick a day, a week or a whole month and dedicate it to providing random acts of kindness. Journal your experiences and reflect on the feeling you received. Harness the gratitude from having the ability to help others.

8.   Bravery and Courage

To be a leader takes bravery. To lead others takes courage. To make this world a better place requires it all. It's not easy to be brave. It's so hard, in fact, that most people would rather live in fear. When you live in fear, you're not actually living. You're in a state of limitation. This world is hard. It's challenging, it's difficult, and it's full of pain. So, it takes a brave person to be happy, joyful, and fight for things that matter in this world.

On the other hand, people with courage are the ones others look up to for inspiration, for hope, for guidance. The thing is: anyone can do it. It just takes having heart; heart enough to do the hard thing. To be the person that's going to stand out in a crowd and go against the norms—go against what's popular—because it's the right thing to do.

You may not be born with bravery or courage, but it can be cultivated. And I promise you, once you get your first taste of freedom—that being brave and courageous gives you—I promise that you will never turn back. Because once you walk this path, you're going to empower yourself and others. Whenever, I feel scared about something I know on the other side of this fear is my liberation. The more you become comfortable with discomfort the easier it becomes.

I invite you to start with baby steps and challenge yourself to do that thing that you've been wanting to do but have allowed fear to stop you. Go take that dance class, ask out that person you've been wanting to connect with, sky dive, or even just start with taking cold showers. Obviously, I don't mean something that is dangerous to your well-being or a discomfort that goes against your values and morals. Just do the thing, you know what it is.

9.   <u>Be Open and Surrender</u>

My openness has afforded me great gifts in life, especially because for most of my life I've been a "control master." A "control master" is a bit more advanced than a control freak. Because of my openness, it allowed me to flow with the adventure of my life. We are in co-creation with Creator and when we are not gripping so tightly to our ideas, we allow the flow of The Universe to guide us.

Being open gives your life room to breathe. It allows for miracles to happen. Surrender, on the other hand, was a greater challenge for me to learn. Being open to goodies and adventure is one thing, but to surrender to things that I didn't want in that moment was extremely difficult. I had expectations for my life; I had things that I wanted to go a certain way. And, when it didn't, it would hurt—a lot. But that's when I learned surrender. Surrender doesn't mean quit or take things lying on your back. It means being in a state of allowing. Trusting that things are not happening to you, but for you. Allowing the moment to be what it is and to not be attached to your idea of what the moment needs to be.

I learned that sometimes you must let go of 'good' things in order for great things to happen. When it comes to the fight or flight response,

I fight. Growing up in my life circumstances I had constantly been living in survival and warrior mode. Which was severely taxing on my nervous system, adrenals and even just my mental and emotional well-being. I've had many sleepless and restless nights. Being in this state of control and allowing my lack of trust to fuel my actions. I tried to force my will to make things happen, which was coming from a state of fear and lack.

Once I learned how to surrender, I learned inner peace. It made the hardships in life not feel so hard. It helped me be O.K. when things didn't go my way. There's a prayer that I learned, called the "Serenity Prayer": "God grant me the serenity to accept the things I cannot change, the courage to change the things I can, and the wisdom to know the difference," which I still do when I need some assistance in helping me to surrender. My belief is that I will always get what's meant for me. So, now I need not worry, or at least I do my best not to, and I stay open and surrender, knowing that everything is working for my highest and greatest good. Believe in yourself and trust your journey.

I invite you to go into nature, sit under a tree and ask yourself "What if everything is happening for me?" and find the golden nuggets of what you're going through right now.

Bonus: Visualize the life you truly desire. Set goals and take divine action. Then let it all go and take it one day, one step and one breath at a time.

Acknowledgements

This book took a village to bring to fruition, and I am eternally grateful for everyone who breathed life into making this book possible. From every person who walked into my life and added to my story, to the people that believed in me. This is a dream come true and a duty assigned to me from Spirit. As you know by now, my life has not been a cake walk. Only with the support of my ancestors, soul family, and Spirit have I not only been able to endure but keep my smile intact. I've walked alone most of my life, but now I know I am far from that. I know just how loved and cared for I am. That is one of the greatest blessings of my life. Without the depths of my darkness and shadows, I would not know the brightness of my light. So, I must express my gratitude for all of those who have broken my heart, especially my mother. For I would not have this incredible depth of love and forgiveness without the lessons these heartbreaks have taught me. I'm grateful for it all.

Thank you all from the deepest part of my heart.

My dad Jerome. Leah, My sister Jericca, my brothers Justin & Kinami, Mama Sarina, Nikola, Kamiko, Neil Glazer and Zahra Dean at Kohn, Swift & Graf. My Ohana: Brooke, Hanna, Ben, Shaun, Dru, Farria, Kapuahinano, Paulina, Delos; Mama Maui for reminding me who I am; Hawaii; Hilaria, Candice, José, Detron, Gabby, Souki, Jtier, Zac, Jenn, Joanne, Elena, Angie, Raean, Mona, Erika S., Erika E., Margot, Alfa, Kathryn, Momo Carebear, Hugo Valentine, Sean Hill, Corbin, Vero, Mitch, Kev, Jamil, Gabrielle, Harry Wan & Suzy Wan; Kombu Sushi family; my therapists Katrinka Terra & Madeline Rodriguez; Mama Pie; The United States Attorney's Office for the Eastern District of New York and the New York Field Office of the Federal Bureau of Investigation. You are all heroes & Earth Angels: Moira, Mark, Tanya, Mike W, Mike, Delise, Charlie, Meagan, Laura, Chris.

Finally…

To "Little Jess" for braving all these storms and keeping your love intact. You have made me who I am and have been my inner light through my darkest of nights. I love you.

Made in the USA
Las Vegas, NV
21 September 2023

77893920R00098

Made in the USA
Las Vegas, NV
21 September 2023

77893904R00098